MOUNT HOOD
EL. 11,245

CRATER
ROCK

SIPPI
HEAD

LONE FIR L.O.

SKI
CHAIR
LIFT
997 FT.

TIMBERLINE CABIN

TIMBERLINE
LODGE

6,000'

TRAIL

TRAIL

TRAIL

ROAD

TIMBERLINE

TIMBERLINE

RIVER

RIVER

SALMON

SALMON

SALMON RIVER

SALMON

EAST FORK SALMON

WEST FORK

EAST
LEG

GARAGE

ROAD

EAST FORK

CLOSED

MOUNT

HOOD

WINTER

WHITE

RIVER

32 MILES
HOOD RIVER

LOOP

142 MILES TO BEND

MOUNT HOOD

A Guide

«*AMERICAN GUIDE SERIES*»

MOUNT HOOD
A Guide

Compiled by Workers of the Writers' Program . Oregon
of the Work Projects Administration
in the State of Oregon

ILLUSTRATED

1940

Sponsored by the Oregon State Board of Control
Co-operating Sponsor,
the Mount Hood Development Association

DUELL, SLOAN AND PEARCE

F
882,
H 85
W 7

OREGON STATE BOARD OF CONTROL
State-wide sponsor of the Oregon Writers' Project

FEDERAL WORKS AGENCY
JOHN M. CARMODY, *Administrator*

WORK PROJECTS ADMINISTRATION
F. C. HARRINGTON, *Commissioner*
FLORENCE KERR, *Assistant Commissioner*
E. J. GRIFFITH, *State Administrator*

23531

6-19-43, Cop/., 75

Foreword

The Mount Hood Development Association takes pleasure in co-operating in the sponsorship of *Mount Hood: A Guide*. In this book the Oregon Writers' Project has prepared a comprehensive handbook and guide to a recreational area that combines the charm and challenge of the primitive with the comfort and conveniences of civilization.

B. UNDERDAHL, *President*
Mount Hood Development Association.

Introduction

AS THE Columbia, greatest of the rivers of the far west, pursues its swift and circuitous course from its source on the western slopes of the Rockies in the remote northern reaches of British Columbia to the Pacific Ocean, it encounters, on the last lap of its journey, four giant peaks, Rainier, Adams and St. Helens to its north, and Hood to the immediate south.

Hood stands right at the notch or gap in the Cascades which the mighty Columbia in some prehistoric age made for itself, that its fast flowing current might escape to the sea. Thus, Hood stands at gaze, the sentinel of the Cascades, its northern slopes washed by the river that has been Nature's master-architect in shaping the contours of the Pacific Northwest. The stream and the mountain are inseparably linked in the minds of the people of this region, who are now engaged in the parallel tasks of harnessing the magnificent power possibilities of the river to their many tasks, while at the same time they are exploring Hood for its recreative potentialities.

Out of this latter endeavor has grown *Mount Hood: A Guide*. The shortening hours of latter-day labor have caused men to turn, as never before, from their engrossing day-long tasks of making a living to out-of-door recreation. In doing so, the people of the Pacific Northwest in general, and those of Oregon in particular, have discovered that the inviting slopes of Mount Hood furnish, to the student no less than to the lover of the out-of-doors, one of the nation's choicest and loveliest playgrounds and study areas, in which the spirit of man, as well as his body, can find re-creation.

INTRODUCTION

Nearly thirty years ago the eminent naturalist, Dallas Lore Sharp, visited the state of Oregon to study its abounding wild life. From this task he was enticed by the ethereal beauty and symmetry of Mount Hood to join a group who made its ascent. As he was resting at the summit, to his great astonishment, he saw that the peak was fairly alive with butterflies. A little investigation disclosed that they were coasting on an up-draft of air from the peak's crater that served them as a toboggan. These fragile creatures had sailed to the top of Mount Hood as to a garden for their play; and there they were, riding their toboggan over and over, apparently enjoying it as much as the skiers of the present day who have found the lower slopes of Hood a perfect playground for their sport.

But if this picture pleased the naturalist who found many other examples (though none so surprising and appealing) of the play instinct, hardly less manifest in animal than in man, Dallas Lore Sharp's love of beauty was gratified most of all by the view of Mount Hood from Council Crest in the city of Portland. A brief quotation from one of Sharp's essays, written, it should be remembered, not by a Westerner boastfully inclined to florid adjectives and purple patches, but by a son of old Massachusetts, may perhaps best serve to conclude this introduction:

"There is one glory of Rainier, and another glory of St. Helen's and another glory of Mount Adams, for these majestic peaks differ from one another in glory, and they all differ in turn from Mount Hood, as Hood, in its difference only, exceeds them all in glory. For pure spirituality, for earth raised incorruptible and clothed upon with the holiness of beauty, Mount Hood, as seen in the heavens from the heights of Portland, is incomparable. As its snow-crowned summit, touched with the warmth of closing day, was first unveiled before me, my soul did magnify the Lord, for the vision, to my unaccustomed eyes, was all divine.

"There are loftier mountains—Rainier and Adams are

loftier; there are peaks that fill with awe and that strike with terror, while Hood only fills the soul with exultation, with the joy of beauty, of completeness and perfection. Hood is but little over eleven thousand feet high, and easily climbed. Its greatness is not physical, not height nor power; but form rather, and spirit, and position. Mount Hood from Portland is one of the perfect things of the world.

"I look down from Council Crest upon the growing city and see the present moment of my country hurried, crowded, headlong. Then I lift my eyes to Hood, serene and soaring in the far-off Heaven, and lo! a vision of the future! not the Mountain that was God, but a summit that is song."

—BENJAMIN H. KIZER

Preface

PAUL BUNYAN, gigantic legendary logger, one July night pitched camp about six strides east of the falls of the Willamette. Here he uprooted with his bare hands a forest of firs and built himself a roaring fire. In the morning, being a worthy woodsman, he covered the embers with a huge heap of rocks and soil and with a final artistic touch sprinkled a bit of snow on the crust. Thus Mount Hood came to be. It's just a pile of dirt. The coals must still glow a little, for there are fumaroles near the apex.

Translated into current measure, Bunyan's strides mean that in sixty and one half of sixty minutes one can drive a distance of 60 miles on a good road from Portland city center, 60 feet above sea level, to the timberline of Mount Hood, 6000 feet above sea level. Almost exactly a mile in elevation above the timberline, or three miles by the perilous trail over the eternal glacier, is the summit. On a clear day it is visible from Portland, where live a third of a million people.

To the Mount Hood area in growing numbers come natives and visitors. They ski, they hike the marked trails, they gamble with death in attaining the very top—and they look and look.

Mount Hood is to Oregon what Fujiyama is to Japan—an oriflamme. It is sometimes said that while the people of Seattle and Tacoma refer to Mount Rainier as "The Mountain," Oregonians speak of Hood as "Our Mountain," a difference in attitude whose significance is patent.

PREFACE

Portlanders have a sort of reverence for their mountain. They build their homes so they can see it. Much as they love trees, they even sacrifice a Douglas fir or two if their view of it is impeded. They point out that nowhere in the world is there a comparable year-round recreation area so close to a large center of population. But this reverence is more than a local tradition. An experienced traveler was seeing the Pacific Northwest for the first time. He stood alone on the balcony at Timberline Lodge, gazing to the south where 52 airline miles away Mount Jefferson centered the horizon and the Three Sisters were dimly discerned in the farther distance. He turned and walked back to the doorway, still silent. Presently he said in a quiet surcharged voice, "It's—it's —"

"Magnificent?" I tactlessly interposed.

"No, it's —"

"Stupendous?" I suggested.

"No, by God, it's wordless."

Yet, although this experienced traveler thinks that the Mount Hood area's beauty defies words, Oregon's forgotten writers have the temerity to try to describe it for you in this little book.

To nature lovers it tells of trails and trees and flowers, of sights and scents, of sports and hostelries, of roads and roads' ends.

Among the many who have helped in the making of it are: E. J. Griffith, State Administrator, Oregon WPA—as a matter of fact the idea originated one day a long while ago when Mrs. Griffith and he sat in the head-house of Timberline Lodge and discussed the need and timeliness of such a book; Mr. A. M. Swartley, Oregon State Mining Board, 329 S. W. Oak, Portland, Oregon; Mr. A. O. Waha, Forest Supervisor, 301 Terminal Sales Bldg., Portland, Oregon; Mr. H. T. Engles, District Ranger, U. S. Dept. of Agriculture, Forest Service, Mt. Hood National Forest, Zigzag, Oregon; Dr. L. S.

PREFACE

Cressman, Museum of Natural History, Eugene, Oregon (University of Oregon); Dr. H. C. Dake, Editor of the "Mineralogist," Portland, Oregon.

T. J. EDMONDS, State Supervisor

Contents

CONTENTS

HIKING AND RIDING TRAILS

xvi

CONTENTS

CONTENTS

Part III, Appendices

xviii

List of Illustrations

xix

LIST OF ILLUSTRATIONS

PHOTOGRAPH BY DONALD G. ONTHANK

Eliot Glacier . . . Terminus of Newton Clark Glacier . . . View of Summit of Mt. Hood from Steel Cliff

PHOTOGRAPH BY COURTESY OF THE OREGONIAN

Climbing Mt. Hood by Way of Steel Cliff . . . Crevasses . . . Ski Tournament . . . Skiers . . . The Ski Jumper Leaving the Take-off

PHOTOGRAPH BY COURTESY OF TIMBERLINE LODGE ASSOCIATION

Riding Party

PHOTOGRAPH BY COURTESY OF U. S. FOREST SERVICE

A Burned-over Area, Mt. Hood National Forest . . . A Stand of Fir, Engelmann Spruce and White Pine . . . Applying Grease Paint to Prevent Sunburning Beaver . . . Building a Fire Line . . . Camping . . . Coyote . . . Mule Deer . . . Punch Bowl Falls, Eagle Creek Trail . . . Sheep Grazing in Mt. Hood National Forest . . . Striped Chipmunk . . . The Expert . . . Tobogganing . . . View of Mt. Hood from Lost Lake . . . View of Mt. Hood and Olallie Butte . . . Zigzag Glacier Prong of Sandy River

———

Timberline Lodge . . . Timberline Lodge, Main Lounge . . . Timberline Lodge, Stairway . . . Timberline Lodge, Typical Bedroom

List of Maps

General Information

Seasons: May to October; summer recreational season. November to April; winter recreational season.

Climate: Summer—Days warm; nights cool. Temperature range, 40° to 85°. Winter—Days and nights cool to cold. Temperature range, 10° to 55°.

Bus Service: Mount Hood Stages between Portland and Mount Hood and central Oregon points. Special all-expense tours in season.

Gray Line Sightseeing Tour: Mount Hood Loop and Columbia River Highway trip, $10, offers close-up view of Mount Hood for about three-quarters of its circumference.

Highways: Bituminous paved highways into the area: from Portland State 50, from Hood River and Columbia River Highway (US 30) State 35 and State 50, from eastern and central Oregon by way of the Dalles-California Highway and State 50 from Maupin Jct.

Traffic Regulations: No fixed speed limit, but no person shall drive at speeds inconsistent with prudent control of car; "indicated speeds," 45 m.p.h. on open highways, 20 m.p.h. at intersections where vision obscured, and 15 m.p.h. passing school grounds.

Parking Areas: Parking not permitted on highways. Parking areas within Mount Hood Recreational Area plentiful. Dur-

GENERAL INFORMATION

ing winter, parking restricted to areas under combined control of state police and forest service.

Service Stations: At frequent intervals.

Accommodations: Arrah Wanna Hotel (*open all year*), 1,300 alt., Wemme; hotel or single room cabins, housekeeping cottages, 2 to 4 persons. Bailey's Mountain Log Cabins (*open all year*), 1,500 alt., Zig Zig; 6 cabins. Battle Axe Inn (*open all year*), 3,888 alt., Government Camp; steam-heated rooms, American plan. Cloud Cap Inn (*open July 1 to September 15*), 5,985 alt., Parkdale; 12 rooms, American plan. Mount Hood Tavern (*open all year*), 3,517 alt., Parkdale; 2 cottages, European plan. Rhododendron Inn (*open all year*), 1,620 alt., Rhododendron; American and European plan. Timberline Lodge (*open all year*), 6,000 alt., Timberline Lodge P.O., 6 *m.* N. of Mount Hood Loop Highway near Government Camp; all rooms with bath, European plan. Numerous improved and equipped forest camps, some with trailer space.

Riding Horses: During summer season riding horses available at Timberline Stables near Timberline Lodge, at Cloud Cap Inn, and at Rhododendron. Rates $3 per day without guide. Pack trains operated out of Cascade Locks on US 30, to Mount Hood and other points of interest on Skyline or Pacific Crest Trail.

Forest Ranger Stations: Zigzag Ranger Station at west entrance to Mount Hood National Forest. Parkdale Ranger Station at north entrance on State 35, 17 miles south of Hood River. Bear Springs Guard Station, on Wapinitia Highway, 25 miles west of Maupin. Beside attending to regular conservation activities and duties as fire lookouts and fire fighters, forest rangers organize rescue parties for those lost or injured in the woods. They enforce forest regulations during summer months and skiing regulations during winter sports season, render first aid and furnish information about trails, fishing, hunting, points of interest, and forest regulations and laws.

Information Service: Zigzag Ranger Station, supplies information concerning points of interest, hunting and fishing, and regulations in area. Service station attendants keep themselves well-informed and are fairly reliable sources of information.

Private Guide Service: Private guides available at Cascade Locks, Hood River and at Rhododendron. Application for guide service should be made well in advance. Fees, $3 to $5 a day.

Special Regulations: Picking wild flowers in Mount Hood Forest is prohibited. Campfires in national forest without written permit from ranger in charge of area prohibited except at public forest camps. During periods of high fire hazard, forest is usually closed to fires of any kind, including tobacco smoking.

Hunting: Licenses required of all persons over 14 years of age. Fees: resident license, $3; juvenile license for those between ages of 14 and 18 years, $1; nonresident license, $15. No closed season on bear or such predatory animals as cougar, bobcat, wildcat, wolf, coyote and lynx. No open season on elk, antelope, or such small fur-bearing animals as fisher, marten, civet cat, ringtail cat, and beaver. Hunting regulations revised every year in July by Oregon State Game Commission. Federal regulations protect certain migratory birds.

Fishing: Licenses required of all persons over 14 years of age. Fees: resident license, $3; nonresident license, $3; juvenile license for persons between ages of 14 and 18 years, $1; special two-day vacation license for resident and nonresident alike, $1. Game fish listed as land-locked salmon, steelhead trout, lake trout, any other variety of trout, and salmon under twenty inches in length. Fishing season varies for certain varieties of fish and for certain streams of area.

Red Cross Service: Red Cross first aid equipment at Government Camp, Summit Guard Station, Ski Bowl, Timberline Lodge, Lone Fir Lookout, and Parkdale.

Ski Patrol: The Mount Hood Ski Patrol, division of National Ski Patrol, organized to administer first aid in case of accident except where doctor is present, carry first aid kits and maintain first aid caches at advantageous places. Patrolmen identified by nickel badge similar to Forest Service shield and labeled "Mt. Hood Ski Patrol," and by orange and black arm brassard. All patrolmen carry standard American Red Cross first aid cards.

Warnings: *To Hikers:* Stay on marked trails; obtain campfire permits if fires are planned. Extinguish all fires after use. Do not drink water from unmarked springs and streams. *To Climbers:* Do not attempt to climb Mount Hood without guide; do not attempt to climb mountain in winter; wear proper clothing; be prepared for sudden extremes in weather; stay with your party. *To Skiers:* Do not attempt ski courses beyond your ability; obey all rules of Ski Patrol; use skis of suitable length; wear proper clothing; call "track" before starting on ski run, and give right of way to those calling for it. Amateurs and beginners should be particularly careful in use of ski poles. Do not attempt prepared "jumps" until qualified to do so. *To Campers:* Obtain camping and campfire permits from Forest Service; carry tools suitable for extinguishing campfires; observe Federal Fire Regulations in force from June 1 to October 31; leave a clean camp. Be sure water supply is pure; signs indicate purity of streams and springs. *To Tobogganists:* All Mount Hood toboggan runs are privately owned. Obey all rules and regulations. Not more than three persons should ride at any one time. No part of body should overhang the toboggan while in motion. Call "track" before starting a run. *To Snowshoers:* Wear rubber shoes with snowshoes. Adjust harness of snowshoe to foot so that ordinary walking step can be taken. Repair immediately any broken portions of web. Exercise extreme care in use of ski poles if carried. *To Autoists:* Do not park on highway. Use chains in winter. Observe all traffic rules and regulations.

Clothing: In summer, prepare for warm days and cool nights. Wear stout shoes for hiking. If mountain climbing is anticipated, wear warm clothing that does not bind, stout shoes or boots with hobnails or climbing cleats and sun glasses. Face should be greased to prevent sun and wind burn.

In winter, prepare for cold weather. Regulation ski suits and boots are recommended if that sport is participated in. Do not wear clothing too heavy or tight fitting.

Summary of Events: Oregon Winter Sports Association sponsors annual winter carnival and skiing tournament. Local ski clubs hold annual ski meets open to public on payment of small fee. Inquire locally about dates and locations.

PART I

Mount Hood's Background

Natural Setting

TO THE Indian, the explorer, and the pioneer, the white peak of Mount Hood was the most distinctive landmark of the Oregon Country. Held in awe by the superstitious red-man, a gleaming discovery to the earliest navigators and pathfinders, and a beacon of assurance to the westward-pushing homeseekers, it symbolized the strength and beauty of an untamed land. Visible from as far east as the Blue Mountains and from as far west as the mouth of the Cowlitz River, it was entered in the records of every prominent early-day traveler by land or by water. It was first sighted in 1792 by Lieutenant William Broughton and named for Rear-Admiral Hood of the British navy.

Mount Hood, in north central Oregon, is most often observed from the west, where it is visible to more than one-third of the state's population. With frosty and imposing dignity it looms above the numerous mountains and foothills that fall away to the wide, populous valley of the Willamette and its northern tributaries. Northwestward from the peak crowd the evergreen-timbered slopes and crags of a rugged and irregular terrain. To the immediate north, wedged like an arrowhead at the heart of the white mountain, Hood River Valley lies tufted with orchards. Coursing from east to west forming the state's northern boundary, the Columbia River cuts a gigantic gash through the massive Cascade barrier. To the east of the mountain the open piney slopes descend to the tawny, semi-arid plains of central Oregon. Southward the forested folds of the Cascade Range extends for nearly 260 miles to the Oregon-California state line. Along this serrated backbone other white peaks stand above the complex topographic pattern of basaltic

3

walls, mountain meadows, glacial lakes, forest-shadowed streams, and waterfalls.

Mount Hood, 11,245 feet in height, is the state's largest mountain, with a basal area of about 80 square miles at the 4,000 foot level. It is in latitude 45°, 22′, 24.3″, and longitude 121°, 42′, 49.6″, and is one of the very few snowcapped peaks in the world that stands alone and visible from every point of the compass.

Portions of the upper reaches of Mount Hood are of broken talus, with steep barren lava outcroppings separating the eleven glaciers. Much loose eroded material, particularly on the west and south sides, coasts down the slopes with the avalanches and melting snows. The soil of the higher altitudes is of the Olympic silt type, in places liberally mingled with sand. Below timberline and common to the adjacent mountains, Cascade silt loam prevails. Annually enriched by decaying vegetation, it spreads into the valleys, fertile and productive. Lava outcroppings occasionally exist as low as the 3,000-foot level. The basaltic dike underlying the Cascadian structure is so deeply imbedded that only the area's deepest stream, the Sandy, has exposed it.

Six rivers and two score creeks carry the melted ice of the glaciers and snowfields to lower valleys. The Sandy River, draining much of the west side, is the longest and deepest of these streams. The narrow canyons of Zigzag and Little Zigzag Rivers course irregularly down the precipitous slopes in a southwesterly direction. Flowing southward are Salmon River and White River, the latter occasionally a tempestuous flood, whitened with lava pumice. East and north of Bennett Pass many tributary creeks feed into the East Fork of Hood River, with the Middle Fork and the North Fork of this stream carrying off the glacial waters of the north slope.

Cascade streams are swift but large waterfalls in the Mount Hood area are few. Widely scattered on the upper slopes of the mountain and usually secluded in forested and fern-clad

4

Lincoln

VIEW OF MT. HOOD FROM LOOKOUT MOUNTAIN ROAD

ILLUMINATION RIDGE AND CRATER ROCK

glens, a number of lakes, notably Bull Run, Lost Lake, and Badger Lake, trap the icy waters from the melting glaciers.

In an area whose contour is marked by many peaks and buttes nearly a score stand out prominently. West and East Zigzag Mountains, southwest of Mount Hood, are scantily wooded knobs almost 5,000 feet in altitude. Slide Mountain, on the upper Sandy River, its barren talus slopes broken and insecure, is almost as high. Bald and Sugarloaf Mountains, and Burnt Peak, which stand to the northwest, and Devils Peak, to the southwest, all approximate 5,000 feet elevation. Ranging eastward along the south skyline are Veda Butte, Eureka and Multorpor Mountains, all on the west slope of the Cascades, and Frog Lake, Bonney, and Barlow Buttes east of the summit. To the north, above Badger and Gunsight Buttes, Lookout Mountain lifts its crown. Between it and the pinnacle of Hood, nine miles to the west, stands Elk Mountain, 5,661 feet in the air; from its northern base stretches the five-mile long, 5,000-feet high Bluegrass Ridge. Lamberson Butte rises against the white eastern shoulder of Hood, but well below the glacial moraine. North of the mountain and beyond Red Hill the narrow Blue Ridge ranges for four miles, a rugged wall between the Middle and West Fork valleys of Hood River. To the northwest, the Sawtooth Mountains form a backdrop for Lost Lake, with Lost Lake Butte on the east. Sentinel Butte and Hiyu Mountain complete a circuit of the most prominent peaks adjacent to Mount Hood itself.

CLIMATE

The climate of the Cascade Range itself is variable, in accord with altitude and season. At the elevation of the Mount Hood Recreational Area (about 5,000 alt.), summer temperatures range from 40° in the early morning hours, to 85° in midafternoon. The winter temperature range is from 10° to 55°.

The Cascade Mountains divide Oregon into two distinct climatic regions: the continental to the east and the marine to the west. East of the mountains rainfall is limited, usually with long moistureless periods during the summer months. In the verdant area to the west, precipitation is liberal in all seasons except summer, when for about three months little or no rain falls. Heavy rains at any time of year are rare, and numerous sunny days enhance all seasons. Thunderstorms, occasionally severe, occur infrequently. There is usually little or no rainfall with these disturbances.

Early fall and late spring rains are common. Chilled by low temperature, these sometimes become sleety and travel must be undertaken with caution. Snowfall is frequent, often storm-driven and heavy during the late fall, throughout the winter, and in the early spring. At extreme altitudes, particularly on the slopes of Mount Hood, smothering storms, sweeping down with little or no warning, are to be expected at any time from October to May. It is characteristic of such storms that they usually cease as suddenly as they strike, followed by clearing weather and sunny days.

For years no official records were kept of the snowfall on Mount Hood, although Mazama climbing parties to the summit have occasionally gauged the snow depths and noted temperatures at varying levels. The Government Snow Course or Snow Gauging Station was established at Phlox Point (5,800 alt.), just below Timberline Lodge, in 1937. The snowfall here is greater than at any similar station in Oregon, and is perhaps as great as at any official station in the United States. Eighteen feet of snow on the level is common at this point. Above at Timberline Lodge during the winter months snowdrifts as deep as seventy feet frequently pile up against the east wing.

Atmospheric conditions in the mountains change frequently. Much of the scenic grandeur and charm of high places is supplied by shifting cloud formations that alter aspects and afford breath-taking backdrops for nature's wild beauty. Cloud masses, white and volatile or cumulus and dark, often obscure the highest peaks and the lowest valleys. Mount Hood frequently disappears and reappears a half-dozen times in a single hour. At times its upper slopes stand above the level cloudfloor that obscures all lesser heights. Fog, too, is common in the fall and summer months and occurs at other times of the year under provoking atmospheric conditions.

In this ancient country there is little change with the years. The attrition of the elements is so gradual that few but the scientist observe the altered aspect; only the occasional avalanche, the displaced rock, the flood-choked watercourse display change. In summer when the snowfields melt back to the parent ice a small shrinkage of the glaciers is noted. A blaze in the timber not immediately controlled may denude some mountain slope, temporarily smudging with black the green mantle. But these scars soon heal. Protected by man in its wildness the Mount Hood area will remain through the centuries much as it is today; as it was before the first road climbed into its high, murmuring silences.

How Mount Hood Was Made

FOR many millions of years two distinct bodies of land, or two islands, rose above the primal sea that covered what is now the State of Oregon. At the close of the Cretaceous period these two land areas were separated by a sea dike which had been slowly rising from the ocean bed from the present Lower California to the Aleutian Islands. Rising slowly this dike, known in Oregon today as the Cascade Range, shut out the sea from the interior and formed three drainage areas. Those to the north were what later became the Columbia Basin and the central basin of southeastern Oregon, whose outlet was cut off and whose waters disappeared through evaporation.

Late in the Oligocene or early in the Miocene epoch of the Tertiary period the vast Columbia lava flows began to well up from the central earth. In this age of volcanic activity the Cascades belched up great clouds of ashes that were carried eastward by the prevailing winds, and spewed out rivers of molten stone that flowed over the face of the land, forming the ocean-like sheets of basalt that cover the region. Twenty-five superimposed flows have been counted along the Deschutes River and the Columbia Gorge. At the close of the Miocene epoch the Cascades presented a range of comparatively low hills covered with dense rain forests, and the region to the east was a land of lakes green with woodlands of magnolia, cinnamon, and fig trees. Sycamore, dogwood and oak flourished, and Sequoias towered to great heights.

During the Pliocene epoch volcanic activity reappeared in the Cascade Range and near the end of the period great ac-

8

tivity in mountain building lifted the range to its great height and erected its jagged superstructure of peaks.

Mount Hood rose in successive outpourings of lava over a period of many eons. Clinkers, cinders, agglomerates and floods of molten lava were spewed forth from the earth vent, and during a long process of building and erosion the mountain grew to a sharp-peaked cone. Its height was probably about 12,000 feet. Horizontal ridges and base spurs developed from the rock slides and flows.

With the close of the second era of vulcanism and the cooling of the peak, heavy snowfalls resumed and glaciers developed on the higher slopes. Gravity carried the ice flows down into the valleys, where they were halted by meeting the warm air of the lower altitudes. The debris borne by the descending ice masses was deposited as terminal moraines. Trees were swept down and buried; some of them, mingled with the sheared-off shoulders of the mountain, are still evident in many places. The slow melting of the glaciers left fan-shaped outwashes as typified by the Zigzag River area. Waters from the upper snow and ice fields began to cut trough-like canyons down the mountain, forming the rivers and creeks of the region, and yearly rains and snowfalls have since kept these streams supplied.

In the process of formation, successive eruptions of the mountain scattered fragments over a wide area, especially to the south. Through long years of erosion only the tougher materials of Crater Rock and the north rim of the original crater, which is now the peak of the mountain, remain. The south wall of the caldera has worn away until little is left to indicate its ancient position. From its former height the processes of glaciation and weathering have reduced the peak to 11,245 feet of rugged grace and white beauty.

Mount Hood, as indicated by various fumaroles and gas vents, is not completely extinct. Rather it appears as a sleeping menace that might be awakened to fury by some future seismic disturbance. Within the crater of the mountain, principally at a point known as the Devil's Kitchen just above Crater Rock, and at inaccessible points on Steels Cliff, are numerous vents from which issue sulphurous gases mingled with water vapor.

Within the last hundred years various demonstrations of volcanic activity on the mountain have been recorded. "It became hot about midday," recorded the *Weekly Oregonian* of August 20, 1859, "and in the evening occasional flashes of fire were seen. On Thursday night fire was plainly visible. . . . A large mass on the northeast side [of Mount Hood] had disappeared, and an immense quantity of snow on the south side was gone." A month later W. F. Courtney, while driving cattle over the Barlow Road, saw "intermittent columns of fire erupting from the crater for two hours." John Dever reported on June 21, 1865, that he had seen "the top [of Mount Hood] enveloped in smoke and flame, accompanied by discharges of what appeared to be fragments cast up from a considerable depth with a rumbling noise not unlike thunder."

Since then no spectacular eruption has been recorded, but as late as 1896 the vents above Crater Rock "smoked and steamed constantly," and "by applying the ear to the ground, boiling and sputtering water could be heard distinctly." In 1935 thermometers inserted in the vents registered 193 degrees F., which is the boiling point at the altitude (10,400 feet). Even today a decided sulphurous odor assails the nostrils of the climber who approaches the fumaroles of Crater Rock and the Devil's Kitchen.

Flora and Fauna

THE Mount Hood area is divided into four biological life zones, with the foothills lying mostly in the Transition zone and the peak mounting through the Canadian, the Hudsonian, and the Alpine zones. Almost the entire range of plant life common to the north Pacific coast is represented in the region. More than 350 species of trees, shrubs, and other plants have been listed as native.

The verdure is the most varied and prolific on the slopes west of the summit of the Cascade Range. The principal tree of this area is the Douglas fir, while east of the divide the yellow or Ponderosa pine is dominant. The heaviest timber growth is in the Canadian and Hudsonian zones, between 2,000 and 4,000 foot altitude, and is principally of evergreen species. Deciduous trees are seldom found above the 3,500 foot level. All growth undergoes marked transformation as it climbs to higher altitudes, where the shorter growing season, colder air, and heavier snows dwarf the size, and the high winds contort the shape. Only vegetation of supreme hardihood endures at 6,000 feet.

Douglas fir, named in 1825 by the English botanist, David Douglas, is common to the whole region and in places stands in almost solid expanse. Not a true fir, its flat, dark-green needles make it readily recognizable. Scattered through the area are the western hemlock, its crowntip always drooping, the white fir, its pale blue-green needles upward and outward curving, and the red cedar pyramidal and dense. Incense cedar with its red deeply furrowed bark is usually found in the lower valleys. Pacific yew grows occasionally near streams and

11

in moist places to timberline. The great silver fir, with grace-ful down-curving branches, ranges from the lower foothills to the higher ridges. Lodgepole pine, high-branched and thin-leafed, grows liberally throughout the Cascades. Formerly the Wasco Indians living east of Hood River floated lodgepole pines down the Columbia for sale to lower-river tribes who had innumerable uses for the straight, slender trunks. Fewer in number but scattered over the whole area are the western larch or tamarack, which drops its scant yellow leaves in autumn, and the noble fir, straight-trunked and tall.

On the eastern slopes of the mountains the dominant tree is the Ponderosa pine, its columnar yellow boles often eight feet in diameter encased in a bark of russet plates from three to four inches thick. Although the western juniper is scattered through the Cascades its favored habitat is these sunny eastern slopes where it seeks exposed places. It seldom exceeds sixty feet in height, its needles gray-green and closely pressed. Here too is the tall slender shaft of the western white pine, its pale bark in sharp contrast to that of the richer Ponderosa.

Unmistakable among the highest climbing trees is the white-barked pine, its snowy trunk glistening in the sun as if ice-coated. This low-branching tree, twisted from constant battle with wind and storm, rarely exceeds twenty feet in height, often being completely covered by the deep winter snows. A prominent species in the higher altitudes is the Alaska cedar or yellow cypress. The Alpine fir lifts tall and narrow amid the other evergreens near timberline, and mountain hem-lock seeks the lofty places. In the high wind-swept spaces that mark the last stand of forest growth the blue-green sentinels of Englemann spruce prevail against the elements, sometimes reaching a considerable height. Their graceful spires are a distinguishing feature of Paradise and Eden Parks and the northside coves.

Although the predominance of tree coverage in the Mount Hood forest is evergreen, numerous deciduous trees intersperse the conifers. In spring the blossom-mantled dogwood spreads a starry constellation against the darker green of hemlock and fir. Chinquapin and alder flourish throughout the region, while here and there on eastside slopes quaking aspen, a member of the poplar family, trembles its silvery leaves. More common is the large black cottonwood or balm. In late summer, most prolific east of the divide, the creamy flowers of the mountain ash become brilliant clusters of scarlet berries. Everywhere are the numerous varieties of willow.

In most sections of the Cascades undergrowth is almost tropical in its luxuriance. Many of the shrubs are annually bright with gorgeous bloom. Red currant, one of the first to bloom, puts forth its flowers before the leaves are fully expanded. Spiraea and syringa, or mock orange, toss white sprays in the sharp sunlight of the openings. On the western slopes in late June the waxen terminal buds of the rhododendron burst open to display large clusters of white and rose and cerise blossoms, almost obliterating the dense dark-green foliage. Other evergreen shrubs are the madrona, a species of arbutus, and wooly manzanita, both with reddish-brown scaly bark.

The fruit of many flowering shrubs was utilized by the Indians in their diet and by the pioneers who succeeded them. Among the most important of these edible berries are the blue huckleberry that grows profusely in the meadows and along the slopes from Mount Hood to Mount Jefferson, the red huckleberry that flourishes in small clumps up to 4,000 feet altitude, and the alpine huckleberry. Another plant especially useful to the Indian was the serviceberry. This plant is the shadbush of New England, the June-berry of the Midwest, the Saskatoon of western Canada. The fruit of this shrub was one of the staples in the manufacture of pemmican, and was also eaten fresh and dried. Lewis and Clark mention a native bread of which the serviceberry was one of the chief ingredients. A famous dish of our pioneer grandmothers was "serviceberry pie." Perhaps the most abundant shrub is the salal, in some places almost the sole forest cover. Its black aromatic fruit is edible but seedy. The Oregon grape, its blossom designated as the Oregon state flower, blooms in early spring and produces a small grape-like berry in late July. The leaves of this shrub closely resemble holly. The reddish-brown thimbles of the salmon berry also ripen in July. The trailing dewberry and the common blackberry form matted thickets in sunny open spaces and in deep shade. The blue elderberry holds its dusky fruit in saucer-like clusters, while the scarlet bunchberry is conspicuous in August on its upright stalk. These plants differ from the poisonous baneberry, whose clustered oval berries, sometimes white, sometimes red, are marked each with a purple spot on the flower end. The small inedible icy-white globes of the snowberry remain thickly on leafless branches well into the winter.

More than fifteen varieties of ferns are native to the northern Cascades. Of these the Christmas or sword fern is the most abundant. Termed an evergreen because of its perennial luster, it grows in moist shady nooks below 5,000 feet altitude. Similar in appearance but taller and more slender is the spike-like deer fern. Both species furnish forage for the deer and elk during the winter months. Familiar on moist banks and rocky slopes is the maidenhair fern, its birdfoot-like black stems seldom growing more than a foot high. Often found as far up as timberline are the tufted cliffbrake, the western lady fern, and the lace fern, while hanging gracefully over broken rocks at high altitudes, is the bladder fern, delicate and tapering and seldom exceeding a foot in length. Licorice fern, creeping over logs and growing trees in damp recesses, has a distinct licorice taste. Growing shoulder high in sunny open places at comparatively low altitudes is the common brake or western bracken. Under a hot sun it exudes a faintly sweet odor.

Many varieties of mosses cling to the rocks and trees of the area, among them the stiff club moss and the running pine moss. The latter is found in open woods creeping over rotting logs and stumps and is often used for Christmas decorations.

Numerous rushes, sedges, and grasses have habitat in the upland meadows. Four varieties of rushes lift stiff, scantily-branching aerials over sandy or rocky declivities. These hollow green stems explode when thrown into the fire—a characteristic utilized by Indian medicine men in treatment of the ailing. Because of the rough surface, pioneers often used the rushes for scouring utensils, guns, and floors. Among the sedges those found at highest altitudes are the northern, the silvery, and the Browers sedge, which wave their coarse grassy branches beyond the last stunted conifers. Other species, light-green or rusty-green, grow at lower levels. Mingling with these are the pale blossoms of cotton grass. Most flowerlike is elk or squaw grass, its large creamy blossoms somewhat resembling spearheads. Squaws used these tough fibers for weaving baskets. Manna grass, a stout handsome species with ample panicles and broad leaves, grows from three to five feet high in moist ground. Nuttal's reed grass is a fibrous tufted variety. Several species of meadow, oat, rye, sheep, broom, and Bent grass are common to prairie and sunny slopes. Formerly purple speargrass grew profusely in Alpine meadows before it was destroyed by grazing sheep. Howell's fescue, also once a luxuriant growth, is now scarcely found except on the talus slopes of the higher altitudes.

Mount Hood in summer is often spoken of as a botanist's paradise, the innumerable flowering plants charming the senses with design and color and fragrance. In densely wooded canyons and high mountain meadows flourish an abundance of alpine and subalpine vegetation, while lower are found the numerous flowers of the more temperate zones.

Since times past hikers along the old Still Creek and Salmon River trails trod in spring over carpets of yellow and blue violets, pink oxalis, golden buttercups, and white linnaea flowers. Through advancing weeks their ways were among waxy white Solomon's seal, purple iris (Iris tenax), pink-tinted bleeding heart (Dicentera), and the tall white and pink foxglove. The skunk cabbage, its showy golden beauty disproving the unlovely name, blooms in boggy places. Here in late May brown-flecked orange tiger lilies nod beneath boughs of plumy ocean spray or arrowwood. The white Mount Hood lily, once profuse in this section, is now scarcely found, having suffered the vandalism of collectors. This and other moist portions south and east of the Sandy River are the natural habitat of three-fourths of Mount Hood's varied vegetation.

Where the mounting trails cross the unquiet streams of June gorged with melting snows, rare "deer's head" orchids, large white moccasin flowers, pale marsh marigolds, shooting stars, and three-leaved anemones or windflowers, in white and shades of lavender and pink, tremble delicately, their blossoms often beaded with moisture. In sparse timber and open fields dogtooth columbines, red, blue, and white, hang their pendent blooms from branching arms. Blue lupines and delphiniums, pink and yellow mountain daisies, and in late summer several kinds of asters and gentians, sway at the edges of the cool canyons and subalpine fields where moisture is fairly constant. Lutkea, a dwarf spiraea resembling saxifrage but related to the rose family, seeks damp shaded places. Many species of cluster lilies abound. White Clintonia or Alpine beauty, blue-fruited when its petals go, blooms beside the creeping dogwood, a mass of foliage and symmetrical white flowers. Mountain torrents are bordered by creeping yellow and crimson Mimulus or monkey flowers.

In the more open timber of the higher forest the large bright yellow daisy-like arnicas and blue larkspurs appear. Great mats of the creeping phlox, with green mossy leaves and starry white, pink, and lavender blossoms, tubular and six-petaled, creep up the sunny slopes as the snow melts. Creamy yellow cats-ear, the flower cup hairy within, lifts in elfin attractiveness from compact, low-growing foliage. July brings the season of bloom to the upper meadows. Numerous varieties of pentstemon or beardtongue, the aristocrats of the heights, nod in the cool breezes. Many species are decked with purple blossoms, others in shades of blue, yellow, and white. The large family of eriogonums, some with close-matted leaves, clutch roots into harsh soil; their gray foliage and bright blossoms of many hues are in places almost the only living color.

Heather displays its greatest charm in the high meadows of Paradise and Eden Parks. The heathers, and the most rare and breath-taking of subalpine flower, the avalanche lily, grow at their best and almost exclusively in these moist areas where snow lies longest. To a slightly less degree the sun-warmed slopes about Timberline Lodge and Cloud Cap Inn are areas of floral color and fragrance. At these places the light gravelly soil below the glaciers runs down into the richer woodland mold where sharply-drained ridges alternate with cool watered canyons. Flowers of the cool northside parks bloom latest.

Eastward of the peak, the yellow pine forests are dry and not very rich in small flowering plants. Still here are found an assortment of pentstemons, eriogonums, phlox, and others of like character. Mahala mat, or squaw mat, is a dwarf creeper bearing dainty balls of lavender that blooms in May and June. Blue and white camas, with hyacinth-like tapering flower heads, crowd the swampy places, principally southeast of Hood, around and below Barlow Butte. The roots of this plant were important in the diet of the Northwest Indians. The giant hellebore lifts its white candelabra at the edges of these marshy places. Red Indian paintbrush, a terminal bracted spike barbarically brilliant, grows in summer throughout the entire Mount Hood area.

When autumn frosts touch Mount Hood's lofty reaches the vivid beauty of the growing season fades rapidly, and is succeeded by the mock brilliance of frosted foliage. Succeeding waves of color, transmuted from flower to leaf, wash down the wide slopes. All deciduous vegetation loses its living green and drops its leaf. In lower forests great-leaved maples stand like glowing golden fires amid the unalterable greens of the conifers. Vine maple in flaming strands creeps through the undercover. Thickets are leaf strewn, the harshness of rock emerges. Again in perennial green the conifers stand, a counter note in the unvarying white of winter snow.

FAUNA

The impression that birds are few in the Mount Hood area is erroneous as many species visit the forested slopes, especially in the summer months, their songs somewhat muted by the vast silences and the great distances. Not all are singers, many game birds and predators inhabiting lofty crags and wooded canyon. Most are summer visitors but some remain the year round.

The high wooded reaches afford an unrestricted flying range for the friendly Clark crow or nutcracker, which launches into swooping flight with a harsh rattling "char-r, char-r." In plumage of brilliant colors the rufous hummingbird, found principally on the west slopes, follows the flowering season up the mountain. In summer bluebirds from dry land areas fly in numbers to the high eastside forests. More beautiful than the brown Oregon vesper swallow, is the blue and white tree swallow which nests in hollow trunks of dead snags. The Western thrush or robin, a summer resident, differs only slightly from the varied thrush or Alaska robin, a shy resident seldom seen. A summer visitor with a particularly lovely song is the yellow-throated Audubon warbler. The water ouzel or "teeter tail" is a small slate-gray bird with a wren-like tail, and although it is not webfooted is an expert swimmer and diver, glibly making its way up the swiftest streams. Its hovering movements over water make it easily recognizable. In the forests the Oregon gray jay comes familiarly about camps and settlements and by its pilfering habits has earned the name of "camp robber." The Stellar jay, mythical demigod of the Chinook tribes, is a familiar sight with his high pointed crest of black and his bright blue coat. White-breasted gray juncos, their tail feathers showing white in flight, are the most common avian inhabitants of the snowy forest. In winter and spring they are companioned by flocks of chickadees and Western evening grosbeaks.

Among birds of prey the bald eagle with clear yellow shanks and white crown, and the golden eagle with plumage of dark brown and lower shank joint feathered, are supreme. These high-soaring birds of the crags at maturity have a wing-spread of nearly seven feet. The sharp-shinned hawk, native and predatory, hovers in the upper air, its underparts white and rusty buff. With head feathers peaked over each ear, the dusky horned owl surveys the nocturnal wilderness from dense high branches. Rather large and powerful, it lives on game birds, rabbits, and small animals and snakes.

Prominent but not numerous among the game birds is the Oregon ruffed grouse, large and brown-mottled with a long black-banded tail. Preferring the mixed woods where streams flow, it flies infrequently and only for short distances. The ringneck or Chinese pheasant is a resident by importation, the male dressed in colorful and variegated plumage. Usually running in coveys, in thickets and meadows, are black-crested mountain quail, small creatures in feathers of slate-gray and chestnut. All of these birds emit startled cries of alarm when surprised or in danger. Band-tailed pigeons, flying in flocks, are seen only on the western slopes. In coloration closely resembling the tame pigeon, they are distinguished by a white crescent on the back of the neck. Loons are rarely seen and the white-tailed ptarmigan or snow grouse disappeared many years ago.

The regions of canyon and deep timber are the favored

habitat of wild game, particularly of the mammals. These creatures vivify the natural scene that otherwise would remain lifeless and inactive except for the movement of cloud and shadow and storm. In recent years, due largely to protective laws, animals in the area have been multiplying in number and are often found by hikers under unexpected circumstances. A few members of the more daring species climb to Mount Hood's very summit.

Of the larger animals members of the deer family, although reputedly wary, are most in evidence. The Columbian black-tailed deer seeks the willow thickets at moderate altitudes, its brownish-gray pelt blending inconspicuously with the dun foliage. The elk or "Wapiti," the great deer of the Oregon country, formerly found in great numbers about Mount Hood, has become almost extinct in the area. It is estimated that sixty elk remain on the upper reaches of the Clackamas River, while a smaller number roam the ridges to the east. The elk is a magnificent animal, a grown bull under wide-spreading antlers standing almost six feet tall at the shoulders, eight feet in length and weighing a thousand pounds. Black bear, awkward and ambling, are often encountered on the north side of the mountain and in the less frequented sections between Summit Meadows and Olallie Lakes.

A few mountain lions or cougars remain in the region. A killer of game, it usually avoids human association. Specimens often attain a length of eight feet from nose to tail-tip. Frequenting deep timber, the Oregon lynx or wildcat grows to a length of more than three feet and to thirty pounds weight. The fur is yellowish-brown often tinged with a russet tone.

Although formerly of ubiquitous presence the great predatory timber wolf is now rare. The coyote, a smaller timorous and sly member of the wolf family, yaps from the eastern ridges.

Lesser animals confined principally to the north side but

VIEW OF MT. HOOD FROM LOST LAKE

U. S. Forest Service

VIEW OF SUMMIT RIDGE, SHOWING SUMMIT LOOK-OUT

Lincoln

VIEW OF MT. HOOD AND OLLALLIE BUTTE

VIEW OF SUMMIT OF MT. HOOD FROM STEEL CLIFF

Onthank

ELIOT GLACIER

Lincoln

VIEW OF CRATER ROCK SHOWING STEAM RISING FROM FUMAROLES

A STAND OF FIR, ENGLEMEN SPRUCE AND WHITE PINE

COYOTE

U. S. Forest Service

STRIPED CHIPMUNK

BEAVER

occasionally seen elsewhere are the Pacific marten or American sable, equipped with slender curving claws for climbing trees. His dark brown body seldom exceeds a foot and a half in length. The Pacific fisher is the largest of the weasels and is a lithe and beautiful creature with fur a deep rich brown. He is an intelligent hunter, loving the night and the mountain marshes where he fishes for frogs, but he is also a swift runner, capturing rabbits and small game. The badger, also of the weasel family, is a burrower with stout digging claws and a squat body and his long stiff grayish coat almost obscures his short legs. Although slow, timid, and wary he is absolutely fearless.

The Pacific beaver is a graceful swimmer and dam builder found in families in the streams and boggy meadow south of Mount Hood. The teeth are broad and chisellike in the small-eared, rodent-shaped head. The largest of the American beavers with body often four feet in length and weighing as much as fifty pounds, this is the prized animal formerly trapped in thousands throughout the Pacific Northwest. Once almost exterminated, it is slowly multiplying in numbers. Not a true beaver, the sewellel or mountain beaver, sometimes colloquially called "mountain boomer," finds his natural abode in burrows in the earth. The short body, brown-skinned and compact, and powerful legs are adapted to digging. Of the rodent family, he resembles the porcupine and marmot rather than the beaver and is only a moderately able swimmer.

The Western yellow-haired porcupine climbs to high altitudes in all sections. The forests everywhere are inhabited by wood rats, cunning friendly creatures familiarly called "trade" or "pack" rats because of a propensity for trading pine cones and such handy objects of no value for the camper's smaller items of paraphernalia. On high rocky slopes lives the pika, little chief hare or "cony"; he has the interesting habit of making hay in summer. The golden mantled ground squirrel or "gray digger" is a destructive rodent seldom climbing beyond low altitudes. Arboreal or tree squirrels are represented by the Cascade pine squirrel or chickaree, in brownish-gray coat, and the large handsome silver-gray squirrel. Chipmunks are numerous and climb to the highest crests, often to Mount Hood's summit. Not a rodent, the Oregon snowshoe rabbit or varying hare has large hairy feet, enabling him to travel over snowy areas. This sprightly creature runs with a bounding hobby-horse movement, is very shy but by the alert may be seen rapidly crossing the high snowfields of winter.

Many streams of the region are spawning grounds for the commercially valuable salmon. Up the Sandy River each spring swim the eulachon or smelt in countless thousands, to reproduce their kind and die in shallow upper tributaries. They are so dense that fishermen take them in nets and buckets. Steelhead trout, renowned for their fighting spirit, are the angler's delight and are found with such smaller trout as the cutthroat, the rainbow, the brook, and the beautiful Dolly Varden. Over one million fish a year are liberated in the streams and lakes of the area.

Many kinds of indigenous fish bait are at the command of the patient angler. Among the ten or more insects the caddisfly is a favorite with trout. Taken from shallow waters, periwinkles, clams, scud, and copepod are prime bait. Four varieties of snails are found in moist places.

Snakes are few and rarely seen and are principally of the garter variety. Rattlers emerge infrequently from among the sun-heated rocks of the eastward foothills.

Summer hikers and campers should be prepared against the clouds of deer flies and mosquitoes that sometimes blow through the still air irrespective of location or altitude. A harmless skin-boring insect of the tick family colloquially called "no-see-ums" occasionally discomfits the visitor. Implausible as it may seem, a species of worm multiplies in numbers in old snow or late-lying drifts, making it generally inadvisable for the climber to use any but lately-fallen snow as a thirst quencher. Honey bees feed avidly on the fireweed, storing their honey in some hollow tree, later to be discovered by the keen nostril of a bear.

During the summer of 1894 Mount Hood's forests were visited by great numbers of white butterflies which destroyed a large percentage of the white-bark pine growth on the north slope. They have not appeared destructively since. Some damage is done yearly, however, by the more than two dozen tree-boring beetles, the hemlock looper or "measuring worm," the silver-spotted pine moth, and the locusts. The latter came in swarms in the early drought season of 1939 denuding portions of the Warm Springs area south of the mountain. Grasshoppers are infrequent visitors and few in numbers. The common blue butterfly which hovers over moist places is not destructive.

History

THE principal Indian tribes of the Mount Hood region dwelt along the Columbia River to the north, the Tygh Valley to the southeast and the Clackamas and Molalla Valleys to the southwest. Small bands of the Clackamas tribe inhabited the area drained by the river that today bears its name, often penetrating to the headwaters on the western slopes of the Cascades. However, their principal village was at the confluence of the Clackamas with the Willamette River. The Molallas, an off-shoot of the Cayuse Indians of eastern Oregon, dwelt in the southern part of Clackamas County and ranged to the summit of the mountains in the region between Mount Hood and Jefferson. The Tygh and the Tilkuni bands of the Tenino tribe, related to the Nez Perces, occupied the valleys of Tygh Creek and White River and the Tygh Prairie about Wapinitia southeast of Mount Hood.

Lewis and Clark recorded that at the mouth of Mosier Creek, near the mouth of Hood River, and a little below Wau Gwin Gwin (Ind. Rushing Waters) Falls, they found villages of the Smackshop Indians. These were what were later known as the Hood River Indians. Concerning Hood River, which they called Labieshe's River, the explorers wrote: "Just above this river is a low ground more thickly timbered than usual, and in front are four huts of Indians on the bank, which are the first we have seen on that side of the Columbia. The exception may be occasioned by this spot's being more than usually protected from the approach of their enemies by the creek and the thick wood behind." On their return up the river in the spring of 1806 they recorded that they stopped

24

at another village of Smackshops near the present site of
Mosier, where they attempted to trade with no success. They
noted other Smackshop villages on the north bank of the river.
The lack of settlement on the southern bank is attributed to
the vicious attacks of the Snakes and Piutes who lived eastward of the Deschutes in south-central Oregon.

The lands of these mid-Columbia people, according to
Lewis and Clark and other early writers, felt the full force
of conflict of three tribal families: the Salish tribes of the east,
the lower Chinook tribes of the west, and the Sahaptin tribes
to the south. According to these writers, from 1750 to 1820
the Snakes and Piutes made frequent raids upon the Columbia
River tribes scattering them and in many cases possessing
their lands. Only the stronger more obdurate bands were able
to withstand the invaders. A few villages, principally at the
"skookum" fishing places, stood after the final raids of the
enemy. Among those able to maintain their stations were the
Wascos and Wishrams at Celilo Falls and the mid-Columbia
tribes, usually by retreating to the north shore when attacked
by invaders. Recent field work has cast doubt upon the state-
ment of these writers that the Piute tribes were in part responsible for these conditions; however, the exact status of
tribal migrations in the section is still far from settled.

The Hood River (Smackshop) Indians, to all intents and
purposes, spoke the same language as the Wascos and Celilos.
This language is identified as the Upper Chinookan or Kikct
dialect. They were related to most of the tribes on the lower
Columbia as well as to the Clackamas and the Clowewalla
and Kushooks near the falls of the Willamette River. Their
principal village was at the mouth of Hood River and was
known as Waucoma, the place of the cottonwoods.

The culture of the Hood River Indians, like that of all the
Chinooks, centers about the river. They are usually called
"canoe" Indians to distinguish them from the "horse" Indians
of the interior. Their houses were usually large wooden build-

ings varying from twenty to sixty feet in length and from fourteen to twenty feet in width. The walls were made of split cedar planks held to upright poles by cords of cedar bark passing through holes in the boards. The roof was made of cedar bark. Along the ridge of the roof an opening two or three feet wide was left to serve as a chimney and to light the interior. The houses were divided into compartments and one house often accommodated a score of families. Fires for cooking and warmth were built in the center of the long house and the beds were arranged along the walls, separated from the main room by mattings. The artifacts of the tribe were almost entirely derived from the forest. Cedar bark fibers were used for mats, capes, and for the strange fringed skirts which was almost the only article of clothing worn by the women in the warmer months. Cedar, fir, hemlock and spruce were used for boxes, bowls, and tubs. Hemlock root and cedar root fibers furnished twine and nets, while grasses and withes were fashioned into baskets and bowls of various design. These people were skilled in basketry and made excellent hampers in which to store pounded fish, pemmican, wappato and other roots, and dried berries.

The principal food of the canoe Indians was the salmon, supplemented by roots, berries and some game. Theodore Winthrop writes in *Canoe and Saddle:* "Salmon netted, hooked, trolled, speared, weired, scopped,—salmon taken by various sleights of savage skill,—is the chief diet. . . . There is exciting salmon-fishing in the turmoil of the rapids. Over the shoots, between boulders and rifts of rock, the Indians rig a scaffolding, and sweep down stream with a scoop-net. Salmon, working their way up in high exhilaration, are taken twenty an hour by every scooper. He lifts them out, brilliantly sheeny, and, giving them, with a blow from a billet of wood, a hint to be peaceable, hands over each thirty-pounder to a fusty attache, who, in turn, lugs them away to the squaws to be cleaned and dried." The chief fishing grounds of the

Hood River Indians were in the lower reaches of the White Salmon and Hood River. The Indian method of preserving salmon was to cut the fish into strips and hang it on scaffolds to dry in the sun. After drying the salmon was pounded between flat stones to a flaky pulp. In this form it was packed in hampers made of woven grass lined with cured salmon skins. Salmon prepared in this manner remained sound and sweet for several years. As such it was an important article of trade as well as food.

The Hood Rivers, with all other Northwest tribes, acknowledged a general belief in an existence after death. They believed in a soul which inhabited the body yet was distinct from the vital principle and capable of leaving the body in dreams and faints. All living creatures were equally endowed, and consequently deserving of respect, and when they must be destroyed, of propitiation by ceremonial address. So it was that the canoe builder addressed the tree as though it were a conscious personality, the fisherman apologized to the first fish of the season as he took it from the water, and the woman spoke deferentially to the cedar from which she took the bark to make her dress.

Speilei, the coyote, and the Thunder Bird were common deities. The Thunder Bird was goddess of the storm, avenger, originator of taboos, and patron spirit of volcanic activity. She made her home in the high crags of the towering white peaks. Speilei, the coyote, in a hundred grotesque forms, was the hero of many stories and the creator of many life forms as well as being the source of rigid taboos concerning food and domestic economy. It was, according to legend, a mighty struggle between Speilei and Wishpoosh, the beaver, that broke through the Cascade barrier and formed the gorge of the Columbia.

Distinction of rank was marked among the tribes and extended even to burial. Slaves were tossed aside or into the river, while the freeborn were carefully prepared for box, vault, tree, or canoe burial and a ritual of mourning exemplified. This took several forms; wailing at specified intervals for a certain period of time, cutting of the widow's hair, and a pious restraining from mentioning the name of the dead.

Memaloose Island, in the center of the Columbia a few miles above the mouth of Hood River, was used as a burial place by these Indians, with ceremonial cleaning and storing of bones. Lewis and Clark called this island Sepulchre Rock and described it thus: "The rock itself stands near the middle of the river, and contains about two acres of ground above high water. On this surface are scattered thirteen vaults, constructed like those below the rapids, and some of them more than half filled with dead bodies." The vaults below the rapids were described as being "formed of boards, slanting like the roof of a house from a pole supported by two forks. Under this vault the dead are placed horizontally on boards, on the surface of the earth, and carefully covered with mats. Many bodies are here laid on each other to the height of three or four corpses, and different articles which were most esteemed by the dead are placed by their side, their canoes themselves being sometimes broken to strengthen the vault." The head of the deceased was usually placed toward the west so the soul might more easily find its way to *Memaloose Illahee,* the land of the dead which lay somewhere toward the setting sun.

The culture of the Clackamas tribe was very similar to that of the Hood Rivers, but that of the Tyghs and the Mollalas differed materially. These latter were more closely related to the "horse" Indians of eastern Oregon. Their houses were of the so-called "pit-house" type which are described as being completely underground. According to the explorers these pit houses were "sunk about eight feet deep, and covered with strong timbers, and several feet of earth in conical form. On descending by means of a ladder through a hole at the top, which answers the double purpose of door and chimney, we found that the house consisted of a single room, nearly circular and about sixteen feet in diameter."

The inland tribes counted wealth in horses and because they were free to move from place to place evolved a culture based on game. Buckskin ornamented with dyed porcupine quills formed their dress, their moccasins, their summer shelters, and skins dressed with the fur intact made their robes and blankets. Game supplemented with salmon, roots, and berries furnished their foods. One of the chief sources of berries of the Tygh and Mollala Indians were the great huckleberry fields on the ridge of the Cascades between Mount Hood and Mount Jefferson. Still the Indians from the Warm Springs Reservation nearby invade this region each summer to replenish their winter supply of berries.

With the coming of the white men and the consequent breakdown of Indian culture, the aborigines slowly unlearned the native customs and the naïve if sometimes unlovely ways of forest and stream. Thereafter, with almost incredible rapidity, they merged into the everlasting twilight of Memaloose, the land of the Indian dead.

As early as 1853 large numbers of Indians from various tribes were gathered together at the Warm Springs Reservation, which lies fifteen miles southeast of the mountain. Herded together in this limited area they wasted away; the Mollalas have vanished, the last of the Hood Rivers have died, and but a handful of a mixed breed of Wascos, Tyghs and Piutes survive under the name of the Warm Springs Indians. The Clackamas tribe, warlike but never large, have long since paddled their phantom canoes into the sunset.

So have passed the tribes that from ancient times dwelt at the foot of the great white mountain. Their tribal signatures, the wilderness trails, remain only in the remotest areas of the evergreen fastness. Marked by the Forest Service as hiking trails, some of them are still in use. From the red Indian past into the white present, they wind threadlike—the almost obliterated evidence of a once proud native habitation.

Lodgefire Myths: Geologists and anthropologists corroborate the symbolism of Indian legends, tales that recall the days when the hero-gods prescribed the limit and expanse of the tides, created the land, and first peopled it with human and animal creatures. As the fiery Thunder Bird flapped her wings and flashed her eyes, mountains rose, volcanoes flared, and seas sank. Coyote and beaver engaged in herculean conflicts, to determine who should be master of the destinies of man. From the Rockies to the Pacific they struggled, releasing the waters of the Inland Sea which followed them down the Gorge of the Columbia.

Passed down from father to son, the tales of these cataclysmic events, taking unto themselves new color and new meaning, became the Indian myths. Through countless ages the story-building elements formed, changed, became blurred, until little remained of their original literalness except a picturesque and exaggerated memory. Around flickering lodge fires the Indians told and retold the story of the creation of Mount Hood, of the five brothers who made the warming Chinook wind, of the magical white elk of Lost Lake, and of the mineral springs with their bitter taste. Five of these legends, closely related to Mount Hood, are here retold in brief.

WHEN MOUNT HOOD SPOUTED FIRE

In the beginning of time when the Inland Sea spread from the Cascades eastward to the Coeur d'Alenes, a proud people lived in the land that stood above the flood. Peace and plenty prevailed, the waters teemed with fish, the forests provided game and the meadows the camas root. In those days when trees, animals, and birds were able to talk like people Koyoda Spielei was their god. He had given the people their mouths and had taught them wisdom.

Dwelling on the western shore of the Inland Sea were the brother mountains, Pa-toe and Wy'east, both of whom loved Beautiful Squaw

Mountain. Now it happened that Beautiful Squaw Mountain grew to love Wy'east, but soon made him jealous by flirting with Pa-toe. The brothers, who were sons of the Great Spirit, soon fell to quarreling, then to fighting to determine which of the two should have her.

They became so angry that from growling and rumbling and stamping their feet they fell to spitting fire and ashes and belching forth great clouds of black smoke. The earth shook and the heavens became darkened. Discarding their white coats, they hurled glowing rocks at each other, painting themselves and the surrounding country with streams of liquid fire.

As this battle raged the forest was burned away, the game killed or put to flight, the fruit and the camas destroyed. The few surviving natives took refuge in caves. Meanwhile in their fighting, the brothers had so shaken the earth that a breach had been torn in the massive Cascade barrier stretching between the two mountains, and through it the vast waters of the Inland Sea had raced downward to the ocean. Over the river, so formed to the westward, a great natural bridge stood.

Among those who had fled into caves for their lives was Beautiful Squaw Mountain. When the rivals came seeking her she could not be found. They were about to resume their vicious assaults upon each other when Koyoda Spielei hurried to the Great Spirit and besought him to come to earth, to rebuke his two sons for their violent misbehavior.

The Great Spirit then decreed that Beautiful Squaw Mountain should remain hidden always and that neither brother should win her affections. He placed a toothless old woman, in the form of a mountain, at the north foot of the bridge that spanned the new river and decreed that the bridge should stand as a covenant of peace between his two sons, and over it the people of the earth should pass to lay their prayers at the feet of the gods. The toothless old woman, he said, would serve as a remembrance that beauty in women is never permanent.

After many lonely years Beautiful Squaw Mountain, guarded by bats placed before the cave by the Great Spirit, stole out of her cavern by night to meet Wy'east. Their meetings, it was said, were not always discreet.

Now it happened that Wy'east was caught one morning, hurrying back from his visit with Beautiful Squaw Mountain across the stone bridge to the south side of the river. But the Great Spirit's wrath was vented, not on the lover but on the bats, which he decreed should thereafter hang head down in caves and places of darkness and fly only by night. He then recognized the loneliness of Beautiful Squaw Mountain and upon her promise not to see Wy'east, allowed her to remain out of her cave.

31

When soon after she and Wy'east asked the Great Spirit's consent to their marriage, he was sympathetic but refused, fearing the rage of Pa-toe. Affairs between the two brothers again became tense. They were held in check only by the words of the Great Spirit. But not for long, for it happened that while he was temporarily away in another part of the world, the brother mountains resumed their hostilities.

Again they hurled forth white hot stones, rumbled, and shook the earth, cast off their white robes and painted themselves with flaming colors. Smoke darkened the skies and the people of the region once more fled to the caves. Game perished in the blackened forests. As the contest raged, the bridge fell in a great mass into the river.

Pa-toe won. Wy'east admitting defeat, released all claim on Beautiful Squaw Mountain. Heartbroken she went to the victor, Pa-toe. At his feet, however, she sank into a deep slumber from which she was never to awaken. She is to be seen today in the Sleeping Beauty, dressed in drab clothes, lying just west of Pa-toe, or Mount Adams. Seeing her fate, Pa-toe who dearly loved her, dropped his head in grief and has never raised it since.

Thereafter Wy'east, or Mount Hood, standing to the south of the river, maintained a proud and defiant silence, which he has never broken. Only in occasional moments of recollection, when smoke can be seen issuing from his hardly-parted lips, does he seem to be pondering a renewal of his wrath.

The old and toothless woman, who guarded the stone bridge, the Indians say, was transformed and became the aloof and beautiful Mount St. Helens.

THE MIGHTY CHIEF AND THE FIRE DEMON

Many, many moons before the coming of the white man, a tribe of mighty warriors roamed the forest-clad hills about the base of Mount Hood. These men were not child-statured as they are now, but were tall as the pines that covered the hills. Their beloved chief, bravest and strongest of them all, was so tall that his tallest subject could easily pass under his outstretched arm. His rule was firm but kindly as he led his people to the best hunting and fishing grounds. His only concern was Sal-leks De-Aubs, the angry demon who dwelt deep down in the bowels of the great mountain. Frequently De-Aubs would throw out fire, smoke, and red-hot whiffs of lava that drove the redmen from their homes. Then the chief would grieve for his people.

One day a dream came to him that unless he conquered the mountain demon and his cohorts, they would eventually cover the entire land with rivers of fire and drive his people forever from the earth. He determined, therefore, to engage De-Aubs and his demons single-handed and drive them from the mountain. After several days of arduous travel he reached the summit. Here he found many large stones. Lifting them, one by one, high over his head, he hurled them down the open entrance that led to the demon's stronghold. Their anger now at a high pitch, the demons heated the stones red-hot and hurled them back at the valiant chief. For many days the battle continued. Desolation spread over the countryside. The din of the conflict was deafening even in far, far places.

Unable to drive the brave chief from the mountain, the demons within it increased the fury of their defense, hurling fire, smoke, and melted rock high into the air. The chief, pausing to see the effects of the struggle upon his people, saw nothing but desolation and ruin. The entire countryside was buried beneath a sea of fire-lava. Gone were the lodges of his people. Gone were the forests. Streams and lakes had disappeared. No living thing was left alive. Dismayed, his great heart broken, the chief threw himself upon the ground and was quickly covered over by the livid streams of molten rock.

Now it happened that a few survivors of this once mighty tribe had taken refuge on the peaks of neighboring mountains. As the earth cooled, following the awful conflict, they returned to their hunting and fishing grounds. Trees, bushes and grasses began to grow again, but they were stunted and sickly. The Indians, too, became smaller and weaker— remnants of the once mighty people. And so they must remain, said the medicine men, until their chief returned to free them from their deformities and to conquer, for all time, the fire demon, Sal-leks De-Aubs. As a sign of his return, the huge shadow of an Indian chief would appear, they said, upon the north slope of Mount Hood. But not until this came to pass would the redmen regain their former stature and strength.

All this happened, the last remembering Indian said, in the long, long past. Today, on the wooded north slopes of Mount Hood there appears, on each afternoon that the sun shines, the enormous shadow-profile of an Indian, each feature prominent, clear cut, and chief-like. Unmistakably, it is the mountain's own shadow, at its best at about three o'clock. As the sun sets its symmetry is spoiled. But the eyes of the native people who read legendary meaning into the shadow no longer gaze southward at the whitened peak from the place Waucomah.

THE WHITE ELK OF LOST LAKE

The mirror lake that lies below the north shoulder of Mount Hood, known as Lost Lake, was not always so-called. Prior to 1880 the few white men who had seen it called it Steelhead Lake, or Blue Lake, mistaking it for that nearby body of water. But the Indians called it Kwoneksamach.

Before the coming of white men, the Indians, threading the Walk Up Trail that ran from The Dalles to the Sandy River, passed the beautiful lake that in fair weather wore like a garland the reflection of Mount Hood. This remote forested area of grandeur and "plenty game," was a favorite feeding ground for elk, and many bands of Indians came here to hunt.

Among the more frequent hunters was a champion killer of the elk. His totem, it was said, was a white elk that accompanied him and on occasions led him to the fattest of the feeding elk bands. This white elk was the Indian's charm of death.

Now it happened that another hunter of considerable might thought to challenge the champion elk killer. He called on the gods of the chase, made strong medicine, and went to the great killing. It was not long before the elk of the region lay dead in large numbers. The challenger had surpassed the champion in slaughter.

This made the champion hunter so angry that he turned upon the white elk and planted an arrow in its heart. Thereupon, the white elk, knowing he had received his death wound, plunged into the lake called Kwoneksamach and, swimming into deep water, began to sink.

When the mighty hunter realized that he was about to lose the white elk, he suddenly regretted his rashness and jumped in to pull the elk ashore and, if possible, to save it. Meanwhile, the rival hunter, seeing the white elk about to drown and covetous of its power, also jumped into the lake to rescue the animal. The three, struggling in the deceptive mirror-like waters, sank into the bottomless depths.

After that—so the tale is told—few Indians would go near the beautiful lake. For years the weird calls of two loons that lived in the reeds by the lake were believed to be the spirits of the drowned Indian hunters.

THE CHINOOK WIND

Various legends have been told of the Chinook Wind, that rises at unexpected times in winters of great cold and suddenly half-strips the peaks of snow, and sweeps bare the low places. Whistling and roaring, this southwest wind melts the surface snows of Mount Hood even at high altitudes. Within as short a time as two hours the thermometer may mount as much as fifty or sixty degrees.

According to the legend five brothers living on the Columbia River east of Mount Hood, were responsible for the friendly and warm Chinook Wind. To the northeast five other brothers controlled the cold and bitter

Walla Walla Wind. The two sets of brothers continually fought each other, sweeping with their strength, first one way and then the other across the country of desert and mountains. They raised great clouds of dust and blew down whole forests. Sweeping into the high Cascades, they heaped up the great snows and in turn melted down the huge drifts.

One day the Walla Walla brothers, jealous of opposition, challenged the Chinook brothers to a wrestling match, with the understanding that the losers should forfeit their lives. This challenge was accepted. Koyoda Spielei, god of all the Indians, agreed to act as referee and to decapitate the defeated adversaries.

Koyoda Spielei went at once to the grandparents of the Chinook brothers, and advised them to smear grease on the wrestling ground that their grandsons might not fall. In like manner he secretly advised the grandparents of the Walla Walla brothers to spread the ground with a sheet of ice.

In the battle that ensued it was almost impossible for anyone to keep upright. However, since it took longer to spread the grease than the ice, the Chinook brothers were all thrown. Whereupon Spielei, according to the terms of the challenge, put the five defeated brothers to death.

Now the eldest of the Chinook brothers had left an infant son at home in his lodge. In due time this son grew to manhood. He vowed to avenge the deaths of his father and uncles. To properly prepare his strength for the inevitable battle with the Walla Walla brothers, he practiced pulling up by the roots tree after tree. Soon he became so strong that he could uproot the largest fir trees and toss them about like straws. He was now ready for battle.

Proceeding up the Columbia River he stopped at the lodge of his grandparents, who, suffering from the tyranny of the Walla Walla brothers, were living in a most deplorable condition. It had been the the custom of these vicious fellows to capture the aged grandfather of the Chinooks, while he fished in the Columbia River, upset his canoe and cause him to lose his fish. On learning this, the young Chinook wrestler instructed his grandfather to fish once again in the river, while he kept a lookout for the Walla Wallas.

As the latter swept down to harass the old man, they were astonished to see the canoe of the fisherman speed swiftly and safely to the shore. All their blowing could not endanger the old man, nor cause his fish to be spilled back into the river.

When the news became known abroad that a new wrestling champion had arisen, the Walla Walla brothers issued a new challenge under the same terms as before. This the young Chinook accepted eagerly, even though he would be one against five.

In the struggle that followed the Chinook wrestler speedily threw each of the first four Walla Walla brothers. Each was in turn beheaded. The fifth, and youngest, however, surrendered without a struggle. Thereupon Spielei decreed that he might live, but that he must be deprived of his power to freeze people to death.

Spielei then ordained that the Chinook champion should thereafter blow upon the mountain ridges first, thus to prepare the people of lower altitudes for his coming. And so has it been since the long ago times.

HOW THE MINERAL SPRINGS RECEIVED THEIR BITTER TASTE

When the years of man's existence counted but few, when the tomahawk was bright with peace among the tribes, there were two brothers. Twins, they were. As they grew to manhood, luck favored one, while the other knew only continual disappointment. As a consequence hatred grew in the breast of the less favored youth. Out of a rancorous spirit he sought to quarrel with his more fortunate brother. Failing in repeated attempts, the embittered one murdered the other as he stooped to drink from a forest spring. He fell into the spring and sank beneath the surface. Immediately great bubbles and gaseous spirits rose from the watery depths and out of a cloud of vapor there appeared an old, old Indian with white hair. He proclaimed himself the creator of the human race, saying, "Accursed of mankind, thou hast sharpened the tomahawk. In its sharpening thou hast unseated sense and embittered man, and strife shall fill the earth as the wage of thy sin. Go! Wherever thou drinkest from a spring its waters shall become polluted."

Through succeeding years the murderer wandered from place to place over the earth. Wherever he stopped to drink at a forest pool there lingered the bitterness of his own lips, and the remembrance of his crime. That was long ago and it was he who gave the taste of bitterness to the mineral springs of Oregon, such as are to be found at places in the Cascades between Mount Hood and Mount Jefferson.

The First White Men: So far as known the first white men to look upon the towering white peak of Mount Hood was the crew of *H.M.S. Chatham* of the British Navy, under the command of Lieutenant William R. Broughton, who sailed up the fabled "River of the West" on October 30, 1792. Entering the river a few months after its discovery by Robert Gray,

SNOW-MANTLED TREES   *Atkeson*

SHEEP GRAZING IN MT. HOOD NATIONAL FOREST

BUILDING A FIRE LINE

MULE DEER

Lincoln

**CASTLE CRAGS AND ILLUMINATION ROCK,
WITH CASCADES IN BACKGROUND**

VIEW OF MT. HOOD FROM ZIGZAG MOUNTAIN
(*Squaw Grass in Foreground*)

Linc

A BURNED-OVER AREA, MT. HOOD NATIONAL FORES

Broughton passed the confluence of the Columbia and Willamette Rivers and reached a point opposite the mouth of the Sandy River. The journal of Edward Bell, clerk of the *Chatham*, records: "We still continued our route, and in the Evening of the 30th we came to a highly sandy point of the River, from whence we had a beautiful view of a very remarkable high mountain, whose summit, and a considerable extent below it, was covered with Snow, and presented a very grand view, this Captn Broughton named Mount Hood." Broughton named the mountain in honor of his patron, Rear-Admiral Samuel Hood.

The first Americans to view the peak from the east were undoubtedly the members of the Lewis and Clark expedition. On October 21, 1805, Captain Clark recorded that "we observed the conical mountain towards the southwest which the Indians say is not far to the left of the great falls. From its vicinity to the place we called it the Timm or Falls mountain." Not until they had passed the mouth of the Sandy River, at the lower gateway to the Columbia River gorge, did they recognize the peak as Broughton's Mount Hood.

Thereafter Mount Hood became a significant geographical feature to the early adventurers into the Oregon country. David Douglas, Captain Fremont, Lieutenant Phil Sheridan, and many others noted its serene sky-piercing loveliness. On some early maps the Cascades are labeled the Presidents' Range and for many years Mount Hood was frequently referred to as Mount Washington. In his *Memoirs* of 1839 Hall Jackson Kelly wrote: "The eastern portion of the region referred to (i.e., western Oregon) is bordered by a mountain range running nearly parallel to the spine of the rocky mountains and to the coast, and which, from the number of its elevated peaks, I am inclined to call the *Presidents' Range*. These isolated and remarkable cones, which are now called by the hunters of the Hudson's Bay Company by other names, I have christened after our ex-Presidents."

Into a region in which even the most important geographic features were inadequately mapped came the fur traders and trappers, the missionaries, the pioneers, the farmers. All vaguely reckoned distance and locality from Mount Hood. In the records, diaries, and letters of many decades there occur again and again reference and tribute to the majestic peak. It was inevitable that the mountain should become the distinguishing landmark of a wide area and should symbolize the spirit of the region. In summation of this attitude John Muir has written: "There stood Mount Hood in all the glory of the alpen glow, looming immensely high, beaming with intelligence. It seemed neither near nor far. . . . The whole mountain appeared as one glorious manifestation of divine power, enthusiastic and benevolent, glowing like a countenance with ineffable repose and beauty, before which we could only gaze with devout and lowly admiration."

Building the Highways: The Cascade barrier was given historic emphasis when the immigrant party of which Samuel K. Barlow was captain starting from Illinois in the spring of 1845, arrived at The Dalles late in September. So far as these pioneers could at first see, this frontier outpost was the end of the westward journey by land; continuation must be by the hazardous Columbia River water route. The excessive transportation charges, the lack of sufficient boats, and the scarcity and high cost of feed determined Barlow to proceed by land. "God never made a mountain without some place to go over it," he said.

On September 24, 1845, the Barlow party, consisting of a train of seven wagons and nineteen persons, wheeled out of The Dalles and proceeded southward along the Deschutes. Crossing the White River, they climbed toward the summit of the Cascades.

Following Barlow's tracks, on October 1, came Joel Palmer, an Indiana farmer with a train of twenty-three wagons. Along

38

the White River, Palmer overtook the Barlow train. Uniting their efforts, the Barlow and Palmer Companies organized for the construction of a roadway over the mountains to the Willamette Valley and the Oregon settlements. For road building work the parties had only axes and saws, consequently much of the necessary clearing was done by burning. Meanwhile, Samuel Barlow and Joel Palmer, scouting ahead, blazed a wagon trail across the divide at a point that thereafter became known as Barlow Pass. Since the season of snowfall was near at hand, it was decided to push through with the company and stock, leaving the wagons behind in a hastily built shelter. One man remained as a winter guard.

A son, Willie Barlow, following an Indian trail to Oregon City secured a packtrain of provisions. Returning, he met the disheartened party struggling through the giant trees and swamps, and over the rough, sometimes precipitate grades. With the weaker of the party mounted, some of them on the backs of cows, but with most of them tramping afoot, the last of the immigrants reached Oregon City on Christmas Day, 1845.

Samuel Barlow petitioned the provisional legislature for the right to construct a toll road around the mountain, over the trail taken by his party. The petition was granted and some money secured to aid in the work. Construction of the road was so far advanced by August 1846 that it was ready for immigrant travel that year. Before snow closed the road "one hundred and forty-five wagons, fifteen hundred and fifty-nine head of horses, mules and horned cattle, and one drove of sheep" had passed through the toll gates, a fee being charged to maintain the road in passable condition. For two years Captain Barlow personally collected toll.

From 1848 to 1862 the road was leased to various operators. These men did little except collect toll and the roadway lapsed into an almost impassable state. In October 1862, the Mount Hood Wagon Road Company, capitalized at $25,000, was organized to reconstruct the way. This work, left incompleted, was taken over by the Cascade Road and Bridge Company in May 1864. Extensive improvements were made in the route; bridges were built and swampy sections of the right of way were corduroyed.

Thus the Barlow Road became the first highway into the Oregon country west of the Cascades, and the Mount Hood region became Oregon's first accessible mountain area, its evergreen gates flung open to coming guests and to eventful history. The construction of this road, wrote Judge Matthew P. Deady, prominent Oregon jurist, some years later, "contributed more towards the prosperity of the Willamette Valley and the future state of Oregon than any other achievement prior to the building of the railways in 1870."

For over a decade the Barlow Road was the only highway into the Mount Hood region. Then in June 1859, an attempt was made by Captain A. Walker and crew to build a road southward from Hood River. It was their intention to cut a route through the forest, following the old Indian Walk-up trail through Lolo Pass to a junction with the Barlow Road near Sandy. However, the venture proved abortive and the road was never finished.

In 1883 another and more successful attempt was made to penetrate the wilderness area to the north of the mountain. Into this region of steep slopes a road-building crew pushed southward, continuing through the summer and into the snows of the autumn. This crude highway, without bridges or established grades, steep and circuitous, was completed the following summer. Over this road the open hacks of the period jolted toward timberline.

In the meantime the old Barlow Road passed successively to the Cascade Road and Bridge Company, the Mount Hood and Barlow Road Company, to be finally bought by Henry Wemme, who in 1912 purchased all right to the road for $5,400. After a few years of operation as a toll road, he opened it to travel without charge, adding greatly to the popularity of the Mount Hood wilderness area. After Wemme's death in 1917, George W. Joseph as his attorney, held the road in trust until 1919, when as Wemme had requested, he deeded it to the Oregon State Highway Commission and the Federal Government, "to have and to hold unto the . . . State of Oregon, with all its mountains and hills, its forests and vines, its flowers and shrubs, its valleys and dells, its rivers and streams, its lights and shadows, its trails and paths, and the beauty and grandeur of Mount Hood, for the use, benefit, and pleasure of all forever."

Agitation for building a modern highway had persisted many years. Finally in 1919, beginning at a point two miles west of Government Camp and including the difficult Zigzag Canyon and Laurel Hill grades, the first Loop Highway work was begun. Sections of the old Barlow grade were utilized. A second work unit soon commenced grading in the upper Hood River Valley. Federal aid was secured and with the assistance of state funds the west leg of the Loop, from Government Camp to the west boundary of the Mount Hood National Forest at Zigzag, was opened in 1920. The Hood River or east leg of the Loop was completed for public use in 1926. A month after its opening it was closed by an August storm that poured a flood down the glacial watercourse of White River. The new highway bridge went out before a great wall of mud and boulders. Before the following spring repairs had been made and the new scenic route was opened to public use and has since been second only to the Columbia River Highway in attraction and appeal.

Trails and Trail Makers: From ancient times an Indian trail passed up Hood River Valley, skirted Lost Lake and climbed over the northwest shoulder of Mount Hood through Lolo Pass to Bull Run Lake, which the earliest pioneers called Chetwood, meaning black bear. From thence it ran to Walker

41

Prairie and the Willamette Falls. This trail coursed generally from the northeast to southwest, and was called by the red tribesmen the Walk-Up Trail. This was later corrupted to Walker Trail. With the coming of white settlers, cattle were often driven over it. John Driver, pioneer stockman, said that he could ride the entire distance on a long summer day. The trail, reaching 4,600 feet altitude, was never popularly used, since it was too steep for wagon travel.

Other trails climbed through the high wilderness of peak and canyon. These were first the paths of the native wild life imprinted by hoof and paw. Over them the elk and deer climbed to the green mountain meadows, munching the chill, harsh grasses as the snows of spring retreated. They were used by the black bear, clumsily ambling forth to feed in the huckleberry thickets. The wolf and the marten and the cougar sped along them to the kill.

But the trails that were ways of life for deer and bear and cougar were also the ways to death, for over them the Indian hunted. Moccasins, deftly placed by speeding feet, marked the trail a little more plainly and padded the rubble-littered path a little more compactly into elemental earth.

From the Barlow Wagon Road many early forest paths climbed to the summit of Mount Hood. Over them settler-guides led an occasional climbing party, indulging a pastime that grew with the years. Among these early trail makers were Perry Vickers (1868), H. C. Yocum (1883), William Gladstone Steel (1883), Francis E. Little (1883), and George Prosser (1885). The first trip afoot around the mountain was made from the north side in September 1892 by G. W. Graham and W. A. Langille, nearby residents.

When in 1893 the Cascade Forest Reserve was created by the Federal government the building of trails to strategic points for fire lookouts greatly stimulated trail development in the Mount Hood area. Old ways were cleared and widened and new routes were blazed. Many of these were opened for hiking and some were marked. Early in the present century several of these forest paths, particularly the Salmon River Trail and the Twin Bridges-Paradise Park Trail, both on the south side, and the Lost Lake-Wahtum Lake Trail on the north side, became popular hiking routes.

In 1897 Elijah Coalman, then only 15 years of age, became Mount Hood's best-known and best-loved summit guide. Making his first climb with Yocum, he thereafter frequently assisted his instructor and was soon leading summit-climbing parties. In 1914 he became a guide for the Forest Service, and although his activities each summer were centered on the snow fields and the peak, where in 1915 he built the lookout cabin, he penetrated much of the wild lower area, blazing and marking trails. Coalman, Thomas Sherrard, and others of the Forest Service, who took charge of the district between 1905 and 1908, gradually developed an elaborate trails system.

Aiding in the early trail building enterprise were the several mountaineering groups that came into being toward the close of the last century. The first of these, the Oregon Alpine Club, was organized in 1887 but soon went out of existence. In July 1894 the Mazamas were organized.

The Mazamas cut new trails and marked old ones, cleared campsites and built shelters. Many of their outing practices were adopted as regulations for the public visiting this and other mountain areas. Much of the work of keeping the trails open has been carried on through the years by this organization, and by other trails clubs of more recent birth, notably the Hood River Crag Rats, the Wy'east Climbers, the Pathfinders, and the Trails Club of Oregon.

When the A. H. Sylvester mapping party of the United States Geographic Survey charted the Mount Hood quadrangle in 1907, they followed many of the early trails. Maintenance work has since occupied much of the time and efforts of the Forest Service. Since 1933, CCC crews have aided materially in trail clearance and construction. In some instances, fire roads have replaced the more important of the early fire trails. At convenient points campsites have been cleared and community kitchens and shelters erected. The trails have been more carefully marked and logged.

Today the entire Mount Hood area is accessible by trail. The traveler may climb to high, tranquil lakes, or to water-falls half-hidden in narrow clefts of the mountain's rocky wall. He may mount canyon ridges, or cross over the bold escarpment of a butte's shoulder to command a sweeping view of vast horizons, of forested hills and snow-clad peaks.

Mount Hood National Forest

MOUNT HOOD stands approximately in the center of the Mount Hood National Forest. Under the authority of the Fundamental Act of March 3, 1891, President Harrison on June 17, 1892, by proclamation, created the Bull Run Timberland Reserve. On September 28, 1893 he added the Cascade Range Forest Reserve. Fifteen years later on July 1, 1908, this area was subdivided into several National Forests, one of which was named the Oregon National Forest. It was from this forest, on January 21, 1924, that the Mount Hood National Forest was carved with a total area of 1,183,765 acres. Within the forest is the "Bull Run Reserve," containing 141,000 acres closed to the public by act of Congress to protect the watershed from which the city of Portland receives its water supply.

The forest covers both sides of the Cascade Range, from the Columbia River to the Clackamas-Santiam divide. It includes 84,258 acres of privately owned lands, leaving a net government ownership of 1,099,357 acres. Almost the entire area is forested with conifers, approximating 22,000,000,000 board feet. Fir species cover the entire western slope, with Ponderosa pine confined principally to the eastern side. The greater proportion of this lumber footage is contained in the Clackamas watershed and the Bull Run water reserve.

Because of its proximity to Portland and the heavily populated north Willamette Valley, the Mount Hood National Forest is the best known of Oregon's thirteen national forests and is the most highly developed recreationally. Its attractions are entirely those of a rough, rugged, mountainous country, of superb landscape and awe-inspiring solitude. Hardly less attractive than Mount Hood itself are the numerous water-falls and the many beautiful lakes within the forest. Alpine meadows, in season gorgeous with color, spread wide amidst the prevailing evergreens.

Within the Mount Hood National Forest, the Forest Service and the State Highway Department have jointly constructed hundreds of miles of motor roads, and have cleared many more miles of trails through dim forests and over steep slopes. Points of picturesque appeal and historic interest have been made available to all. The Forest Service provides numerous convenient camp sites and adequate shelters, and owns and supervises the operation of the mountain's most recent and most impressive man-made landmark, Timberline Lodge. Constructed in 1936 and 1937 by the Works Progress Administration, the Lodge stands high on the south slope of Mount Hood. Elsewhere among the great trees, are nine other lodges and taverns, privately owned, and hundreds of summer homes erected by Oregon citizens. Ski trails and areas developed and supervised by the Forest Service lead down the snowy grades and over the winter-whitened landscape.

All of the resources of the Mount Hood National Forest—recreation, timber, water for irrigation and power, wild life and grass—are managed under a multiple-use plan, which coordinates and systematizes the utilization of each resource so that the entire forest contributes to the social and economic welfare of local communities, the state, and the nation.

Over 384,800 people, using more than three million gallons of water daily, comprising the population of the cities of Portland, Oregon City, Cascade Locks, The Dalles, Gladstone, Gresham, Dufur, Corbett, and Rhododendron drink water from streams rising within the Mount Hood National Forest. Bull Run water is bottled and sold for domestic and office use in many Pacific Coast cities.

Supplying 7,335 persons living on 1,771 farms covering

40,469 acres, water from streams and lakes within the forest is carried through pipes and ditches to lands adjacent to the Forest boundary. This use of water for irrigation purposes is carried on in co-operation with local associations of farmers, state projects, and Federal bureaus.

Electric power companies using hydraulic energy whose source lies within the Mount Hood Forest develop a total of 90,825 KW, and supply electricity for light, cooking, and water heating to 60,513 homes. Hydraulic power plants are at Casadero, Bull Run, River Mill, Tygh Valley, and Cascade Locks.

Owing to the fact that privately owned stands of timber are more accessible to market than those found in the Mount Hood National Forest, cutting to date within the area has been limited. The total volume of timber cut within the past ten-year period totals approximately 130,000,000 board feet, with a stumpage value of over $170,000. Future cuttings will be on a basis allowable under sustained yield management. A total of nearly 7,000 acres has been planted with young trees. Of this, 2,797 acres were on old burns which had failed to reforest naturally, and 4,128 acres were formerly private lands cut over and later acquired by the United States. Plantings now range from three feet to thirty feet high and are almost entirely Douglas fir.

In the more open timber stands, particularly in the Ponderosa or yellow pine area on the east slope of the Cascade Range, a valuable undergrowth of herbaceous and shrubby vegetation is found. This comprises the important food plants for big game animals and domestic livestock. Summer range, which is important to the profitable operation of the stock raising industry, is utilized by nearby stockmen. About 2,000 head of cattle and 20,000 head of sheep are given yearly pasturage. A program of conservation preserves the forage crop. Management of the range is regulated in a manner to assure the continued enjoyment of other forest uses. Soil erosion and water losses are minimized by a program of control.

47

Fire is by far the greatest enemy of the forests, although insects and disease including beetles and white pine blister rust, annually take their toll. From 25 to 30 per cent of the Mount Hood Forest area was devastated by fire before the present system of national Forest administration and protection was inaugurated in 1905. These early fires left innumerable dead trees standing and a heavy accumulation of debris which, together with the steepness of the slopes and adverse weather conditions later prevailing, made fire fighting extremely difficult. For years roads and trails within the area were few, and protection facilities were limited. As a consequence additional acreage was burned over. Later years, however, show a marked decrease in fire losses, in spite of a tremendous increase in the number of forest users. This has come about through increased funds and additional protection facilities.

The availability of CCC and other emergency workers during the past five years has made possible an extensive protection and improvement program. This program, operative at the present time, includes road and trail building, the stringing of telephone lines, the development of fire breaks, and the construction of lookout houses, towers, and other structures. All endangering debris is being cleared. CCC men are trained and effectively used in fire prevention and fighting activities. As a result, the fire losses during the past five years have been very small. An average of only 21 acres of the National Forest land has been burned over annually—a loss of 46,000 feet, board measure, an average total damage of a little over $700.

All of the activities within the Mount Hood National Forest are controlled and supervised by the Forest officials, acting for the Federal government.

In 1931 the Forest Service set aside part of the north and west slopes of Mount Hood as a primitive area, to be preserved as nearly as possible in its natural state. The Mount Jefferson

Primitive Area embraces a portion of the Mount Hood Forest to the south, largely in the Clackamas watershed.

The Mount Hood Recreation Area, which includes a wide stretch on both sides of the Loop Highway from Zigzag Ranger Station to a point just beyond Polally Forest Camp on the north side, was created and defined in 1926. Within the limits of this extensive section the mountain's recreational activities are centered and the major sports' accommodations have been made. The Recreational Area comprises approximately one-fifth of the Mount Hood Forest acreage.

PART II

Tours And Trails

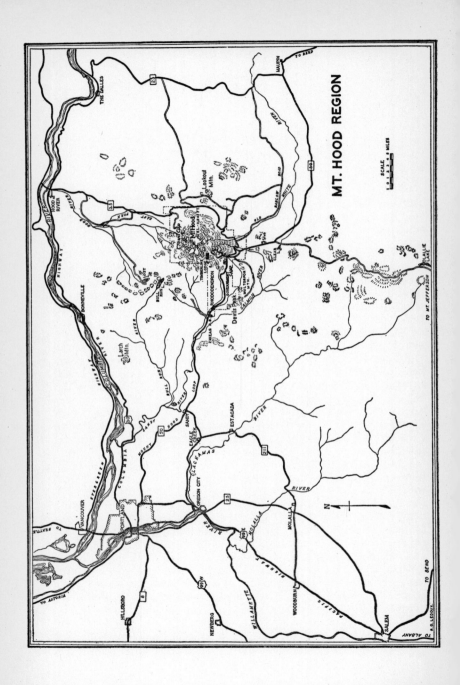

MT. HOOD REGION

SCALE
0 1 2 4 6 MILES

Motor Tours

TOUR 1

Portland—Sandy—Zigzag Ranger Station—Government Camp
—Timberline Lodge Junction—Timberline Lodge; 64.2 m.,
State 50.

Bituminous macadam pavement.

State 50, the southern leg of the Mount Hood Loop Highway, leaves PORTLAND 0 m. (69 alt., 301,815 pop.), by way
of the Ross Island Bridge and Powell Valley Boulevard and
winds southeastward through areas of suburban homes and
berry fields to GRESHAM, 14 m. (295 alt., 1,635 pop.), site
of Multnomah County Fair, and to SANDY, 25.8 m. (1,012
alt., 234 pop.), entrance to the Mount Hood region.

ZIGZAG RANGER STATION, 43.7 m. (1,400 alt.), Forest Service
headquarters for the district (camp fire permits and general
information), is at the west entrance to the MOUNT HOOD
NATIONAL FOREST (see Mount Hood National Forest).
Just north of the highway is the confluence of the Sandy and
Zigzag rivers. The Sandy was first named Quicksand River by
Lewis and Clark in 1805 when they explored the region near
its mouth.

RHODODENDRON, 45.7 m. (1,600 alt., 50 pop.), named
from the profusion of the blossoming shrub, is a community of
summer homes and commercial resorts. (Hotel; cabins; service
station; tourist supplies.) Just east of Rhododendron is a junction with the PIONEER BRIDLE TRAIL (see Hiking and
Riding Tours), which follows the old Barlow Road and
roughly parallels the highway to Government Camp.

TOLL GATE FOREST CAMP, 46.5 m., is at the side of the old
Barlow Road tollgate. Over this road and through this gate
came many of the early settlers of the Willamette Valley and
of western Washington. The road was first traced by members
of the pioneer wagon train of 1845, who endured much hard-

53

ship and suffering in the journey. In 1848 it was made a toll road by the provisional government. A toll of $5 for each wagon and $1 for a single head of stock was levied. After two seasons, considering himself repaid for his outlay in building the road, Barlow relinquished his control of the highway to the territorial government and for a time it was free of toll. Later Foster and Young rechartered the road as a toll road.

A building of shakes, the third tollgate structure on the old road, still stands at the old site. The original building was burned many years ago. A large corral stood near by.

At 48.8 *m.* is a junction with a forest road.

Right on this road to CAMP CREEK FOREST CAMP, 0.3 *m.* (2,100 alt.), an entry point for the Pioneer Bridle Trail and start of Still Creek Trail (*see Hiking And Riding Tour No. 5*).

THE OREGON TRAIL TAVERN, 51 *m.*, is a commercial resort. On the walls of the foyer hangs a picture of the original Barlow Tollgate building.

At TWIN BRIDGES FOREST CAMP, 51.3 *m.* (2,907 alt.), is the start of the Paradise Park Trail (*see Hiking and Riding Tour No. 6*).

From BARLOW FOREST CAMP, 52 *m.* (3,000 alt.), Hidden Lake Way leads (L) upward to Timberline Cabin and the snout of Zigzag Glacier (*see Hiking and Riding Tour No. 7*).

LAUREL HILL, 52.6 *m.*, was the most dreaded portion of the pioneer trail. The wagons were let down by means of ropes snubbed to trees and some of the rope burns made in this procedure are still on the older trees. Another method of braking the descent was by means of trees tied to the rear of the wagons and dragged along the ground. One pioneer wrote: "we went down Laurel Hill like shot off of a shovel." In 1853 E. W. Conyers wrote in his diary: "The road on this hill is something terrible. It is worn down into the soil from five to seven feet, leaving steep banks on both sides, and so narrow that it is almost impossible to walk alongside of the cattle for any distance without leaning against the oxen. The emigrants cut down a small tree about ten inches in diameter and about forty feet long, and the more limbs it has on it the better. This tree they fastened to the rear axle with chains or ropes, top end foremost, making an excellent brake."

A local legend about "the treasure of Laurel Hill" is current. Two outlaws quarreled over their spoil while en route to

Portland over the old Barlow Road. On Laurel Hill the quarrel culminated in the death of one of the robbers. The other buried the gold beneath the body of his companion at the foot of a huge pine, and fled on to Portland where he obtained work, married and settled down. Perhaps it was fear of the place where he had committed murder but he never returned to the spot where he had buried his stolen wealth. Just before his death he told the story to his son and described to him the location of the cache. The son spent several summers in vain endeavor to find the treasure. He found the large pine blazed as his father had described it but no bones or money lay at its base. The marks of the digging are still discernible. Perhaps somewhere on Laurel Hill is a lonely unmarked grave and beneath it bags of gold.

At 53.2 *m.* is the start (R) of the Yocum Falls-Mirror Lake Trail (*see Hiking and Riding Tour No. 8*).

From the SUMMIT OF LAUREL HILL, 53.5 *m.* (3,425 alt.), is a beautiful view of Mount Hood which looms cameo-like against the northeast horizon. On the slope of Laurel Hill a short distance from the lookout is an old apple tree thought to have been planted by a pioneer or to have grown from seed dropped by an immigrant on the old road.

At 54 *m.* is an extensive parking space from which a trail leads (R) to the Ski Bowl, the Slalom Course and the Tom-Dick-Harry Mountain Ski Racing Trail (*see Winter Sports and Ski Trails*).

GOVERNMENT CAMP, 56 *m.* (3,870 alt.), was so designated when a detachment of Federal soldiers was forced to abandon its wagons here in the winter of 1849. The military train was in command of Lieutenant William Frost. The place was at first spoken of as "the government camp in the mountains." At Government Camp are several hotels, stores, and service stations, which cater to the visitor at all seasons of the year. A resort hotel begun by O. C. Yocum in 1900 was the nucleus from which grew the present settlement. In 1911-12 Elijah Coalman, the noted Mount Hood guide, erected the first "Government Camp Hotel." Taking over the Yocum homestead of 160 acres, Coalman set up a portable sawmill and manufactured the lumber for his hotel. The building was three stories high with a steep pitched roof designed to more readily shed the heavy snows. Coalman who preferred guiding to the confinement of inn-keeping sold the business in 1914.

For years Government Camp Hotel was the only lodge on the south side of the mountain. From it were made the first ascents of the southern slope of the mountain. The hotel was destroyed by fire in October 1933.

BARLOW MONUMENT, 56.1 *m.,* commemorates Samuel K. Barlow and his wife. Declaring that God never made a mountain without leaving some place to go over it, he and his companions sought out a way to cross the Cascades and thus shun the perilous boat trip down the Columbia River from The Dalles.

SUMMIT GUARD STATION, 56.6 *m.,* is the forest ranger station for the Government Camp area. From the guard station the Skyline Trail leads southward along the summit of the Cascades (*see Hiking and Riding Tour No. 10*).

At 57 *m.* is a junction with a forest road. Left on this road to SWIM and SHERAR BURN (*see Motor Tour 5*).

From TIMBERLINE LODGE JUNCTION, 58.2 *m.,* the route leads over the east leg of Timberline Lodge Road to the timberline of Mount Hood.

TIMBERLINE LODGE, 64 *m.* (6,060 alt.), is a long low hotel and recreational center on the south slope of the mountain (*for rates see General Information*). The lines of the great irregular structure harmonize with those of the peak behind it. The lodge is unusual in that its design, construction, and ornamentation are the result of the skills and passionate devotion of many different kinds of people. Just as the building of a medieval cathedral became a labor of love in which each artist, mason, architect, glassblower, weaver, and patron endeavored to express his religious devotion by turning wood, stone, flax, wool, glass, and paint into a thing of supreme beauty, so the WPA workers, architects, administrators, and sponsors endeavored to make Timberline Lodge express their love for their beautiful mountain.

The individual type of architecture, called Cascadian, is an excellent example of the adaptation of design to use. Against a background of rugged beauty the building rises in an epitome of the over-towering peak. The hexagonal central unit is dominated by a huge chimney with three fireplaces in the main floor lounge and three more in the ground floor ski lounge. From it extend two wings in which are dining rooms, guest rooms, and dormitories.

The interior decorations and the furniture of the lodge are

... our full range at www.TwoBadMice.com ·

motivated by the Indian, the pioneer, and nature. Figures of mountain creatures are carved on the newel posts of the great stairway. On one crouches a badger, on another a bear while on others are a beaver, a squirrel, an eagle and wild fowl. The andirons in the room fireplaces are wrought in the form of beavers, squirrels and other forest animals. On the walls of the guest rooms are water-color sketches of wild flowers and plants indigenous to the Mount Hood region. Draperies and rugs are hand-woven and of primitive design.

Views from the lodge are superb. Immediately to the north looms the massive white crest of the mountain in jagged contours against the intense blue of the sky. Southward across a billowing forest of dull green lift the peaks of Mount Jefferson, the Three Sisters, and lesser crests. Eastward stretch the dun-colored uplands of the Inland Empire, while westward like a hazy cloud low on the horizon the Coast Range edges the shores of the Pacific.

TOUR 2

Portland—Eagle Creek—Hood River—Mount Hood—Junction State 50; 112.8 m., US 30 and State 35.

Concrete and bituminous macadam pavement.

US 30, the Columbia River Highway, leaves PORTLAND, 0 m. by way of Burnside Bridge and Sandy Boulevard and, passing through a region devoted to dairying, bulb culture and general farming, enters the Columbia River Gorge, which it follows to Hood River. Winding around the face of the bluffs, dipping to the margin of the river, again mounting the sheer wall to neighbor with the white falling water of a dozen cascades, the road is considered one of the most scenic highways in America (see OREGON: END OF THE TRAIL, Tour 1). For almost twenty-five miles it traverses the northern edge of the Mount Hood National Forest.

From EAGLE CREEK FOREST CAMP, 44.2 m., the Eagle Creek Trail leads southward past Lost Lake to the Mount Hood Primitive Area. Eagle Creek Camp is one of the favorite picnicking spots in the Columbia Gorge Park.

The COLUMBIA GORGE RANGER STATION, 49.8 m., is the headquarters of the Mount Hood National Forest. This point is

57

the northern terminus of the Oregon Skyline Trail which follows the backbone of the Cascade Range the entire length of the state.

HOOD RIVER, 67.9 *m.* (100 alt., 2,757 pop.), is the northern gateway to the Mount Hood region. It is the seat of Hood River County and shipping center for a world famous fruit producing section. Great warehouses and canneries for processing the products of the Hood River Valley line the railroad tracks. A trim business district occupies the flat bottom land of the Columbia River while residences line the wooded streets along the sharply rising slopes of the valley. During the fruit season the population of the town is augmented by the many additional workers who come into the valley to harvest the crops. The presence of these migrants quickens the social and economic pace of the town and adds materially to its life and color. The Indians of the area called the site of Hood River Waucoma, the place of the cottonwoods. These trees grow in abundance in the vicinity and in spring the fuzzy down of the cottonwood blossoms are an annoyance to housewives. The Indians say that this fall of the cottonwood bloom always means the annual freshet of the Columbia River has passed its crest.

Southward from Hood River State 35, which the route now follows, traverses the famous Hood River Valley fruit growing district. The altitude of the valley gradually rises toward Mount Hood and is hemmed in by spurs of the cascade Range which give it the form of an oblong bowl. The huge bowl is divided into two smaller bowls by BOOTH HILL, the terror of travelers in the early days of wagon transportation.

MOUNT HOOD (P.O.), 81.4 *m.* (1,467 alt., 65 pop.), was so named because a magnificent view of the mountain towering against the southern sky is obtained at this point.

DIMMICK STATE PARK, 82.9 *m.* (*camp grounds and tables*), is a wooded area of eighteen acres.

At 83.6 *m.* is a junction with a macadam road.

Right on this road to PARKDALE, 0.3 *m.* (1,700 alt., 125 pop.), distributing point for the upper valley and center of the fruit packing industry for the neighborhood. Strawberries are an important crop and a strawberry festival is held in early June. Although in recent years they have been mostly replaced by white workers, Indians from the Yakima and Warm Springs reservations formerly were the principal berry pickers. While the squaws and papooses gathered the fruit, the bucks for the most part slept by day and gambled or disported in tribal dances at night.

Even today a few Warm Springs Indians frequent the berry fields at picking time and it is no uncommon sight to see a squaw stooping along the rows with her small papoose strapped to her back.

West of Parkdale to LAVA BEDS, 1.6 *m.*, an area of tumbled and broken scoria about a half mile in width and four miles in length extending along the Middle Fork of Hood River. From it flow a number of fine springs.

Northern entrance to MOUNT HOOD NATIONAL FOREST is at 90.9 *m.* Here in magnificent display is an epitome of the forests of Oregon. Douglas fir, hemlock, noble fir, white fir, yellow pine, tamarack, lodgepole pine, cedar, spruce, maple, alder, intermingle in a green expanse that rolls across ridges and canyon in almost unbroken phalanx. Undergrowth is almost impenetrable, rhododendron, spiraea, oceanfoam, and a myriad of wild flowers bloom in season.

At 91.7 *m.* is a junction with the Cooper Spur road.

Right on this road to HOMESTEAD INN, 1 *m.* (3,775 alt.), a log hotel with adjoining log cabins (*American plan, 20 rooms*). Winding up the northwest flank of the mountain the road climbs over 1,200 feet in six miles to a LOOKOUT POINT, 7.1 *m.*, that affords an excellent view of the Hood River Valley, the Columbia River, and an extensive panorama of mountains.

At 9 *m.* is a junction with a graveled road.

Left on this road to TILLY JANE FOREST CAMP, 1.5 *m.* (*tables, stoves, etc.*), focal point of the Cooper Spur skiing area. Near Tilly Jane camp is the base camp of the American Legion of Hood River which sponsors an annual climb to the summit of the mountain, usually by the Cooper Spur of the Sunshine route (*see Ascent of the Peak*). At the end of the Cooper Spur Road is CLOUD CAP INN, 10.5 *m.* (5,985 alt.), erected in 1889 of Amabilis fir logs. Designed to harmonize with its setting of stunted pines, crags, and snowfields it was opened in August of that year and has since been operated each season from July 1 to September 15 (*accommodations for 30 guests*). Constructed in a day when the land lying between the forks of Hood River and the North side timberline was wilderness, this lodge and the road leading to it were the earliest developments of the Mount Hood recreational area. James L. Langille of Hood River was in charge of construction with work-gangs made up principally of Chinese laborers. The building is anchored to the basalt spur by cables to keep it in place during winter storms. The inn is situated directly below the snout of Eliot Glacier about three miles from the summit of Mount Hood. From this point ascents are made to the peak of the mountain. Owners and builders were William S. Ladd, Portland banker, and Colonel C. E. S. Wood, lawyer and poet. It was designed by the architectural firm of Whidden and Lewis of Portland. The Inn was purchased by the U. S. Forest Service in 1940.

South of the Cooper Spur Road, State 35 enters the canyon of the East Fork of Hood River, which it follows for several miles.

Just south of the Polally Creek is the POLALLY (Ind. sandy or powdery) FOREST CAMP (R), 94.3 *m.*, and at Trapper Creek crossing is the SHERWOOD FOREST CAMP (R), 96.3 *m.* Paralleling Blue Grass Ridge (R) for several miles the highway winds southward beside the white glacial waters of Hood River.

One of the mysterious characters of the Mount Hood region was Wheelbarrow John, who appeared in the 1880's. If he had any other name it was never known. He was rarely seen since he traveled mostly at night, at which time he was glimpsed, usually trundling his belongings up the East Fork of Hood River as far as the roads and trails would permit. It was supposed that he was prospecting the east side of the mountains, and there were times when the evidence of such an activity was found. The few ore exposures he left showed very low values, and he seemed not to tarry very long at any one spot. He disappeared as strangely as he came.

At 98.3 *m.* is a junction with a mountain road that leads eastward toward Dufur and The Dalles (*see Motor Tour 8*).

HORSE THIEF MEADOWS (R), 99.4 *m.* (3,550 alt.), was named for an outlaw who had a cabin near by. In the summer of 1884 a man who called himself Phillips came to Hood River Valley and hired Dave Cooper to aid him in the search for a cabin under the floor of which, he declared, there was hidden a cache of $25,000 in gold. He said the money had been taken in a stagecoach robbery near Walla Walla, Washington, a few years before. The search was continued for two years when the cabin in Horse Thief Meadows was found; but if any money was recovered Dave Cooper never received a share. The old cabin still stands and is pointed out in corroboration of the story.

ROBIN HOOD FOREST CAMP (3,560 alt.), is at 99.9 *m.* (*Information on trails and camps may be obtained at the Double Three Forest Service Station.*) The Badger Lake Trail leads eastward toward Gumjuwac Saddle (*see Hiking and Riding Tour No. 16*).

HOOD RIVER MEADOWS AND FOREST CAMP, 103.8 *m.* (4,480 alt.), is on the southeast shoulder of the mountain. Almost surrounded by the slender spires of the pointed firs the grassy meadow in summer lies studded with hundreds of mountain blossoms of white and red and orange and blue, patterning the grassy expanse into a tapestry of variegated design. Right

from the meadows the Cold Springs Creek trail winds northward along Blue Grass Ridge (*see Hiking and Riding Tour
No. 14*).

SAHALE FALLS (Ind. supreme) 104.4 *m.* (4,575 alt.), is a
graceful cascade near the highway (R) on the headwaters of
the East Fork of Hood River. (*Drinking fountain.*) It was
named by George Holman of Portland in a contest seeking
an appropriate name.

From BENNETT PASS, 105.3 *m.* (4,670 alt.), is a magnificent
view of the crags and glaciers of Mount Hood (R) looming
against the sky. A mountain road leads eastward from the
pass toward Lookout Mountain (*see Motor Tour 8*). Bennet
Pass, although the highest point on the Mount Hood Loop,
is not the dividing summit of the Cascade Range but of a
spur that reaches eastward between the Hood River and White
River drainage areas. It was named for Samuel Bennett, an
early day Wasco County stockman.

At 107.2 *m.* is the IRON CREEK FOREST CAMP.

WHITE RIVER FOREST CAMP, 107.5 *m.*, is on the bank of the
turbulent White River which heads in White River Glacier
on the southern slope of Mount Hood. In midsummer the
river, fed by the melting snows of the peak, often becomes a
raging torrent of milky white glacial silt.

At 109.2 *m.* is a junction with the Barlow Ridge Trail (*see
Hiking and Riding Tour No. 13*).

BARLOW PASS, 109.9 *m.* (4,158 alt.), is significant in the
settlement of Oregon. Through this pass poured the thousands
of pioneers eager for new homes in the green land of the
Willamette Valley. But if it was a way of hope it was also a
way of privation and hardship. One who experienced the
ordeal wrote: "Some men's hearts died within them and some
of our women sat down by the roadside—and cried, saying
they had abandoned all hope of ever reaching the promised
land. I saw women with babies but a week old, toiling up the
mountains in the burning sun, on foot, because our jaded
teams were not able to haul them. We went down mountains
so steep that we had to let our wagons down with ropes.
My wife and I carried our children up muddy mountains in
the Cascades, half a mile high and then carried the loading
of our wagons up on our backs by piecemeal, as our cattle
were so reduced that they were hardly able to haul up our
empty wagon." (*See History.*)

Southward from Barlow Pass leads the old immigrant road laid out by Samuel Kimbrough Barlow and Joel Palmer in 1845 (*see Motor Tour 7*).

From BUZZARDS POINT, 110.8 *m.* (4,000 alt.), is an expansive view of mountains, forest, and meadows. In the foreground are Salmon River and Summit Meadows with the tree-clad Cascade Range stretching away to the horizon culminating southward in Mount Jefferson and northward in the tall white majesty of Mount Hood.

At 111.8 *m.* is a grave marked simply "In Memory of a Pioneer Woman of 1845." The original burial place was in the center of the highway. When the highway was put through, the grave was removed to its present site. It is of a mother who had almost attained to the dreamed-of country when stricken at the gate. Her husband made a coffin from a wagon box, the iron parts of which were found by the road construction crew.

At 112.8 *m.* is a junction with State 50, the Wapinitia Highway (*see Motor Tour 3*).

TOUR 3

Junction State 23—Bear Springs—Blue Box Summit—Junction Timberline Lodge Road; 40.8 m., State 50, The Wapinitia Highway.

Bituminous paved roadbed.

The Wapinitia Highway is the main entrance from central Oregon into the Mount Hood Recreation Area. Crossing a high and arid Juniper Flat studded with scraggly growths of juniper, sagebrush and stunted pines, the road enters the Ponderosa pine belt which it traverses for many miles to a junction with the Mount Hood Loop Road on the south slopes of the mountain. The first part of the route passes through the region formerly claimed by the Tygh Indians (*see History*). The area, devoted principally to stock raising, is settled sparsely.

From a junction with State 23, 0 *m.*, three miles west of Maupin, State 50 enters Juniper Flat.

At 7.4 *m.* is a junction with a dirt road.

Left on this road to WAPINITIA, 1 *m.* (2,023 alt., 35 pop.), a small dry-land village, and into the WARM SPRINGS INDIAN RESERVA-

TION, 4 *m*. The reservation of 300,000 acres was set aside by the Federal government in 1855. Through treaties negotiated by General Joel Palmer, superintendent of Indian affairs, members of the Tenino, Wasco, and Piute tribes were placed here. The reservation was named for the Warm Springs River which was named for the many warm springs on its banks. The population of the reservation is 992. The Federal government maintains a boarding school for the Indian children. A small public school is maintained for the children of white employees of the agency.

SIMNASHO (Ind. cor. *Simnassa*, thorn bush), 12.7 *m*. (2,357 alt., 25 pop.), is a center of Indian activity on the reservation. These activities include the annual root festival in the spring when the roots become edible. This occurs about the time of Easter but is a tribal celebration. A like event is the berry or harvest festival held after the huckleberry crop is gathered. Tribal dances are also given occasionally, when many beautiful costumes are displayed.

WARM SPRINGS, 32.8 *m*. (1,535 alt., 50 pop.), is administrative headquarters for the reservation. (*No public accommodations at the agency. Visitors welcome and may secure meals at the Government Employees' Club. No liquor allowed on the reservation.*)

West of the junction State 50 leaves the sagebrush uplands and enters the belt of yellow or Ponderosa pine characteristic of the eastern slope of the Cascade Range. However, toward the summit the open stands of the huge russet-boled Ponderosa give place to the denser growths of fir and hemlock.

THE MOUNT HOOD NATIONAL FOREST is entered at 18 *m*. At BEAR SPRINGS, 21.8 *m*., is an improved forest camp.

Left from Bear Springs a dirt road leads southward into the Warm Springs Reservation, 4.7 *m*., and past HE HE BUTTE, 12.5 *m*., where there is an Agency sawmill.

At 26.9 *m*. is a junction with a dirt road.

Left from this junction over a forest road to a junction with the Skyline Road, 5.5 *m*. (*see Motor Tour 6*).

At BLUE BOX JUNCTION, 32.9 *m*. (3,750 alt.), is an intersection with the Skyline Road (*see Motor Tour 6*).

BLUE BOX SUMMIT, 34 *m*. (4,024 alt.), is the highest point on the route.

FROG LAKE (R), 34.7 *m*. (3,872 alt.), is a small scenic lake nestled among evergreen forests. Here is the FROG LAKE FOREST CAMP.

Right from Frog Lake to the FROG LAKE BUTTES LOOKOUT, 3 *m*. (5,342 alt.).

WAPINITIA PASS, 35.2 *m.* (3,931 alt.), is the dividing ridge of the Cascades.

Passing through a heavily forested area State 50 traverses the SALMON RIVER MEADOWS and crosses the EAST FORK OF SALMON RIVER, 39.5 *m.*, and the WEST FORK, 39.7 *m.*, to a junction with State 35, 40 *m.*, (R) a part of the Mount Hood Loop Highway (*see Motor Tour 2*).

West of this junction State 50 leads along the south base of Mount Hood. At 40.8 *m.* is the junction with the east TIMBERLINE LODGE ROAD (*see Motor Tour 1*).

TOUR 4

Zigzag Ranger Station—Old Maid Flat—Clear Fork Guard Station; 4.4 m., Clear Creek Road.

Dirt road; some grades.

The Clear Creek Road winds northward from ZIGZAG RANGER STATION, 0 *m.* into the Bull Run Reserve. Up a gradual grade the road climbs through an area of summer homes, one of the best developed sites of the Mount Hood area.

At 0.2 *m.* is the ZIGZAG CCC CAMP (R) and at 0.6 *m.* the entrance to the MOUNT HOOD NATIONAL FOREST. CLEAR CREEK FOREST CAMP, 1.8 *m.* (1,600 alt.), is picturesquely situated among evergreens.

As the road mounts along the valley between the Sandy River and Clear Creek frequent glimpses of Mount Hood may be caught between the towering eastward peaks of ZIGZAG and SLIDE MOUNTAINS. Ahead loom SUGARLOAF and NORTH MOUNTAINS. Although much of the adjacent territory is eroded and seamed with crags, scattered forest growth prevails.

At 3.1 *m.* is a junction with a side road.

Left on this road along the course of Clear Creek to the entrance of the BULL RUN RESERVE (*closed to the public*), 2.4 *m.* (2,475 alt.) an area about the headwaters of Bull Run River for the protection of the Portland water supply. BURNT PEAK rises loftily ahead.

Winding eastward across OLD MAID FLAT, 3.3 *m.*, the road follows the north bank of the Sandy River to the CLEAR

Fork Guard Station, 4.4 *m.* (1,950 alt.), at the edge of Bull Run Reserve.

TOUR 5

Junction State 50—Sherar Burn—Kinzel Lake; 8 m., Sherar Burn Road.

Dirt road; some steep grades.

Sherar Burn Road leaves the Mount Hood Loop Highway (State 50) 0 *m.* just east of Government Camp near the Summit Guard Station and curves southwestward around Multorpor Mountain through a rugged region of forests and tumbled peaks.

SWIM, 0.3 *m.,* is a small resort at the east base of Multorpor Mountain.

Near Swim is the STILL CREEK FOREST CAMP, 0.5 *m.* (3,760 alt.).

SUMMIT MEADOWS, 1.5 *m.* (3,650 alt.), is the site of the first tavern on this section of the old Barlow Road. In 1868 Perry Vickers built a cabin and trading post which he called Summit House. For many years it was a convenient stopping place; the keeper often assisting and housing "movers" without pay. As a member of the posse pursuing a bandit Vickers was killed in 1883 at the White River Crossing a few miles to the east. After Vickers' tragic slaying Horace Campbell, a religious eccentric nicknamed "King David," rebuilt the Summit House and constructed in the rear a building in the form of an Indian teepee, conical in shape with a central fireplace and a "smoke-hole" at the peak. Near the site of the old Summit House is a small graveyard where Vickers and travelers who died en route through the Cascades lie buried. Beside Vickers in the cemetery is the grave of a small child, the infant son of "W. and L. Barclay" who died at the age of two months at the Meadows in 1882.

Southwest of Summit Meadows the Forest Service road passes through scattered reproduction of Alpine hemlock, Douglas fir, noble fir, and Western red cedar and Alaska cedar.

At 3 *m.* the road skirts EUREKA BUTTE (R) and at 3.7 *m.* VEDA BUTTE (R).

FIR TREE FOREST CAMP, 3.8 *m.,* is at the head of the small but turbulent Fir Tree Creek.

Right from Fir Tree Forest Camp a trail leads to lovely VEDA LAKE, 1.2 *m.* (*camp grounds*).

At 4 *m.* the SHERAR BURN is entered. Rhododendron, chinquapin, squaw grass, tiger lily and many other flowers make masses of color in season. Beginning at 4.5 *m.* the road follows a jagged ridge with an average altitude of 4,000 feet, Mount Hood continuously in view along the northern skyline.

KINZEL LAKE, 8 *m.* (4,300 alt.), is a small blue medallion nestled among the evergreen forest at the foot of Devils Peak. On the shore of the lake is KINZEL LAKE FOREST CAMP.

Right from Kinzel Lake to the DEVILS PEAK LOOKOUT STATION, 1.5 *m.* (5,054 alt.) from which is obtained a magnificent view of Mount Hood and the surrounding mountains.

TOUR 6

Blue Box Junction—Clackamas Lake—Warm Springs Meadow —Lemiti Butte—Olallie Meadows—Olallie Lake; 35.5 m., The Skyline Road.

Graded summer road.

This summer motor route (*open July 15 to October 1*) winds along the crest of the Cascade Range, crossing and recrossing the divide, in close proximity to the Oregon Skyline or Pacific Crest Trail. From its junction with State 50 at BLUE BOX JUNCTION, 0 *m.* (3,750 alt.), the Skyline Road winds through Alpine forests past CLEAR LAKE BUTTE (R) (4,440 alt.), and NORTH GATE, 3.8 *m.* (Guard Station). Here the Forest Service maintains a gate and watchmen to insure that travelers do not use the road until sufficiently dry in summer to insure safe travel.

BIG MEADOWS, 8 *m.,* is one of the numerous upland prairies wedged between walls of blue-green forests on the west slope of the Cascades. Near CLACKAMAS LAKE, 8.3 *m.* (3,337 alt.), is the CLACKAMAS LAKE RANGER STATION and CLACKAMAS LAKE FOREST CAMP.

At 14 *m.* the road recrosses the rugged summit of the Cascades to the east side. South of WARM SPRINGS MEADOW, 20.2 *m. (shelters)* the road crosses once more to the west side and weaves through alternate stretches of meadow land and forest. PEAVINE MOUNTAIN, 23 *m.* (4,893 alt.) rises abruptly ahead with PINHEAD BUTTE, 24.2 *m.* (L), overshadowing the route. LEMITI BUTTE, 27.7 *m.*, crowds the road to the east while SISI BUTTE (5,614 alt.), is high on the western skyline. In this region deer and bear walk boldly from the forests that margin the meadowlands. Beavers are occasionally seen in the icy creeks that meander through the harsh grasses.

From beautiful OLALLIE MEADOWS, 31.4 *m.*, and the OLALLIE MEADOWS FOREST CAMP, the motor road runs southward and skirting the western foot of OLALLIE BUTTE (7,210 alt.), enters a region of a hundred lakes that lie scattered on both sides of the Cascade divide. At the crest of the range is OLALLIE LAKE, 35.5 *m.*, the largest of these lakes and the center of the Olallie Lake Recreational Area, the southernmost in the Mount Hood Forest. Swimming, fishing and boating are available to the vacationist (*cabins, supplies, saddle horses, boats*).

From this point roads and trails lead southward into the Willamette National Forest and the Mount Jefferson Primitive Area.

TOUR 7

Barlow Pass—White River Crossing—Bonney Meadow—Junction Bennett Pass Road; 18.5 m., old Barlow Road—Bonney Butte Road.

Dirt surface mountain road; some steep grades.

Branching southward from the Mount Hood Loop Highway (State 35) at BARLOW PASS, 0 *m.* (4,155 alt.), the old Barlow Road winds southward around the western shoulder of BARLOW BUTTE, 0.5 *m.* (5,035 alt.), and for a distance of eleven miles closely parallels Barlow Creek. Over this trail, blazed in 1845 by Samuel Barlow and his wagon train poured an unending stream of pioneers eager to reach the green lands of the Willamette Valley. The DEVIL'S HALF ACRE, 1.5 *m.*, is a meadow marsh profuse with such Alpine flowers as the marsh marigold, buttercup, Indian paint brush, yellow musk, and blue erigerons. Here also are a number of dams constructed by the energetic beaver. Close by is the DEVIL'S HALF ACRE FOREST CAMP.

From the Devil's Half Acre a Forest Service fire road leads southwest to the BEAR SPRINGS FOREST CAMP, 7 *m.*, on the Wapinitia Highway (*see Motor Tour 3*). This affords an attractive loop trip return to Government Camp.

WHITE RIVER CROSSING FOREST CAMP, 9.5 *m.*, is at the point where the old Barlow Road crosses the turbulent milky waters of White River, one of the difficult spots on the trail.

At 10.5 *m.* is a junction with the Bonney Butte Forest Service road. From this point the old Barlow Road leads eastward down the valley of White River to TYGH VALLEY and the Dalles-California Highway (State 23).

Northward from the junction the Bonney Butte Road winds along the east slope of BONNEY BUTTE RIDGE to BONNEY MEADOWS, 17 *m.* at the foot of BONNEY BUTTE (5,593 alt.). At the edge of Bonney Meadows is BOULDER LAKE FOREST CAMP on the shores of a small mountain lake. Just north of the lake is a large mountain known as CRANE PRAIRIE.

At 17.5 *m.* is a rough mountain road.

Left over this road to BONNEY BUTTE LOOKOUT STATION, 0.5 *m.* The road, although steep and over rubble, is safe and the lookout station affords a splendid view of the surrounding country. Southward across the deep White River Canyon several major peaks of the Cascade Range are visible. To the northwest looms Mount Hood, gigantic and deceptively near. Eastward the great interior wheatlands stretch out into a giant checkerboard such as the mythical Paul Bunyan might have used to while away his leisure hours.

North of Bonney Butte the road passes through a somewhat open country with scattering forests of balsam fir, hemlock, and spruce. Beside the road bloom many Alpine flowers, especially the St. John's wort. Numerous birds and small animals are often seen along the route.

At 18.5 *m.* is a junction with a fire road leading to Lookout Mountain (*see Motor Tour 8*).

68

MOTOR TOURS

TOUR 8

Bennett Pass—Gunsight Butte—Gumjuwac Saddle—Junction Dufur Road—Junction State 36; 19 m. Lookout Mountain Road—Dufur Road.

Mountain road; winding, some steep grades.

Branching eastward from BENNETT PASS, 0 *m.* (4,670 alt.), on the Mount Hood Loop Highway (State 35), the Lookout Mountain Road leads through a forested area of balsam fir, mountain hemlock, and Alaska spruce. At 3 *m.* the country becomes more open and many Alpine flowers, principally St. John's wort, bloom beside the way.

At 4 *m.* is a junction with the Bonney Butte Road (*see Motor Tour 7*). Northward from the junction the Lookout Mountain road leads through an open range country along a sharp ridge. Stands of Ponderosa pine, spruce and fir are traversed. Deer, bear, rabbits and grouse may often be seen in passing. Luxuriant growths of mountain flowers; blue erigerons or asters, Indian paint brush, pentstemon, and many others color the ground in season.

At 6 *m.* the highway crosses the trail to BADGER LAKE (*see Hiking and Riding Tour No. 14*).

At 8 *m.* the road crosses GUNSIGHT BUTTE (5,990 alt.), and at 9.5 *m.* passes through GUMJUWAC SADDLE (5,730 alt.). In this area are encountered pure stands of western larch, a characteristic timber of the east slopes of the Cascades.

At 11 *m.* is the junction with a dirt road.

Right on this road to the summit of LOOKOUT MOUNTAIN, 1 *m.* (6,525 alt.), where the Forest Service maintains a lookout. This peak commands a view of seven snow capped mountains. Close by to the west is Mount Hood while northward across the Columbia River in Washington are Mount Adams, Mount St. Helens and Mount Rainier. Southward along the Cascades are Mount Jefferson, Mount Washington, and the Three Sisters.

From the base of Lookout Mountain the road runs almost due north along the hogback of a sharp ridge to a junction with the Dufur Road at 15 *m.* Left on the Dufur Road to the Mount Hood Loop Highway (State 35) at 19 *m.*, a mile south of SHERWOOD FOREST CAMP (*see Motor Tour 2*).

Hiking and Riding Trails

TOUR 1

Welches—Salmon River Guard Station—Linney Creek Forest Camp; 12 m., The Salmon River Trail.

The Salmon River Trail parallels Salmon River through a deep canyon shaded by forests of Douglas fir, Western red cedar, white fir, bigleaf maple, alder, and western yew. Shrubs and flowers are not plentiful except on side trails into more open country, but tiger lilies, bleeding hearts, columbines and other common species thrive in season.

The route, leaving State 50, 0 m., follows the Welches Road past TAWNEY'S, 7 m., to a gate into the MOUNT HOOD NATIONAL FOREST, 2.1 m. At this end of the road, 2.5 m., the Salmon River Trail leads left. At 3.5 m. is the lower SALMON RIVER FOREST CAMP (*picnic facilities*). Swimming in the "Big Hole," half a mile above the camp, is available to those who enjoy a cold plunge. The SALMON RIVER GUARD STATION, 5 m., issues campfire permits and maintains a camp ground nearby.

Leaving the Guard Station, the trail swings around the side of a steep rocky bluff a hundred or more feet above the river. The trail drops down to the level of the river at 5.9 m. and at 6 m. (R) crosses over foot log to ISLAND CAMP.

At 7.1 m. is the ROLLING RIFFLE FOREST CAMP and the BIGHORN FOREST CAMP (*shelter cabin, camping facilities*) is at 7.4 m.

The river now enters a deep gorge and the trail climbs along the hillside. Maidenhair fern is abundant. At 9.5 m. the route breaks out of the timber onto a rocky knoll. From this vantage point there is a splendid view of the deep gorge (R) and the forest-clad hills to the south. The trail continues through open country to LINNEY CREEK FOREST CAMP at the confluence of Salmon River and Linney Creek.

TOUR 2

Rhododendron—Tollgate—Laurel Hill—Government Camp;
11.5 m., Pioneer Bridle Path.

Easy grades and a broad trailway make the Pioneer Bridle
Path a popular route for the horseback recreationist who
wishes to remain near to the highway at all times. From
RHODODENDRON at Vine Maple Road, 0 *m.*, the trail
climbs eastward, paralleling CAMP CREEK (R), to the TOLL-
GATE FOREST CAMP (L). From there on its way is between the
Loop Highway on the L. and the creek. At 0.5 *m.* is the SITE
OF THE OLD TOLLGATE HOUSE. Within the first mile three
streams are bridged. A rocky area is traversed at 1.2 *m.*

Beyond a new bridge, 1.5 *m.*, the trail penetrates the brushy,
young forest of vine maple, alder, and Douglas fir that is
typical of this area. At 2.4 *m.* is a summer home road and
2.7 *m.* is (R) CAMP CREEK CAMP (*shelter*). The "Bridle Path
Caves," 3.2 *m.*, is so named for the density of the timber at
this point.

The Bridle Path, using portions of the OLD BARLOW ROAD,
climbs through an alder and maple slashing, 5.2 *m.*, and at
6.4 *m.* mounts a rocky ledge, with Camp Creek brawling
noisily far below (R). An old gold mine shaft, 6.5 *m.*, is a re-
minder of early and unprofitable attempts at mining.

At the BARLOW FOREST CAMP the Pioneer Bridle Path
UNDER-PASS, 7.1 *m.* dips under the Loop Highway at its turn
around and over Laurel Hill (R), the grade of great hardships,
down which at its highest point the pioneers came on their
way into western Oregon. Up to this point portions of the
trail are miry until midsummer, but the entire route is always
negotiable by the mounted traveler.

The trail mounts to the LAUREL HILL RIDGEWAY that separates the highway from the LITTLE ZIGZAG CANYON (L).
Picturesque view points, looking both north and south, are
afforded. The Bridle Path, which runs generally parallel with
the highway and to the north of that artery, again approaches
it closely and at 9.3 *m.* joins it. The path continues beside
the road (L) through wind-bitten shrubs and scattered clusters
of evergreens to GOVERNMENT CAMP, 11.5 *m.*

TOUR 3

Rhododendron—Lookout Cabin—Old Barlow Road—Zigzag
Ranger Station; 10.5 m., West Zigzag Mountain Trail.

This route, with an unobstructed mountain view for 80 per
cent of its distance, follows Henry Creek Avenue (one half
mile east of Rhododendron), 0 m., to the junction point of
Rhododendron Way, 0.5 m., which bears northeast. The trail
climbs through a heavy forest of deciduous trees, among them
being vine maples, and red alders. Pheasants and chipmunks
are commonly seen. At 1 m. the trail emerges from the timber.

Two fires have burned over Zigzag's rocky south side in the
past twenty-five years, leaving many bleached tree skeletons.
In this open area flowers and shrubs have since flourished.
Squaw grass and ocean spray intermingle with red huckleberry and chinquapin. This is a steep area and for the first
three miles the trail climbs steadily, but is readily traveled by
the average hiker.

At 1.6 m. seen eastward across the valley of the Zigzag River
(R), appear the odd-shaped CASTLE ROCKS. Drinking water
may be obtained from springs at 2 m. and 2.4 m.

There is a short cut (L) at 2.4 m. up to the west Zigzag
Lookout Station, but the trail proper intersects (L) at 3 m.,
where the phone line crosses and Zigzag Way becomes the trail
route. Mount Hood stands plainly to view in the northeast.
Douglas firs, Western hemlocks, lodgepole and white pines,
and noble firs are scattered along these higher levels. The trail
proceeds at easy grades. The white caps of the Cascades—
Rainier, St. Helens, Adams, Hood and Jefferson—are all visible from WEST ZIGZAG MOUNTAIN (4,500 alt.), LOOKOUT
CABIN, 3.7 m., on a day of clear visibility. This emergency
Lookout Station is occupied only in extremely hazardous fire
weather. (*Visitors will please refrain from disturbing any
Government property.*) Cliff swallows, hummingbirds, red
shafted flickers, and juncos seen here seldom rise above this
altitude.

At 5.1 m., near old SNAG CAMP, rhododendrons and squaw
grass are especially bountiful from June 10 to August 1.
Columbine, tiger lily, phlox, gentian, snowberry, and many
other flowers grow profusely here. A spring provides drinking
water. At 7.3 m. is another spring.

The Zigzag Mountain Trail drops down the west slope to the ZIGZAG RIVER ROAD, 9.6 *m.*, which it follows (L) to the TRUMAN ROAD, 10.3 *m.* The route emerges at the Loop Highway (State 50) at ZIGZAG, 10.5 *m.*, in a rocky area just east of the river's confluence with the Sandy River. Salal, manzanita, elderberry, and vine maple are overshadowed by the commoner evergreens and big leaf maples.

TOUR 4

Junction State 50—Devils Canyon—East Zigzag Mountain—Paradise Park; 10 m., East Zigzag Road and Trail.

Leaving the Loop Highway (State 50), 0 *m.*, over the Enola Hill Road, this hiking or riding route proceeds to the Zigzag Mountain Road, 1.4 *m.*, which winds abruptly east and north to a terminus in DEVILS CANYON, 3.4 *m.*

DEVILS CANYON VIEWPOINT (3,050 alt.), affords a splendid view of Devils Creek Falls (east), the tip of Mount Hood (northeast), and Devils Peak (south). The canyon of the Zigzag River, picturesque and deeply evergreen, sweeps eastward to distant Barlow Camp on the highway.

Here the Zigzag Trail begins, climbing along the high east side bench of EAST ZIGZAG MOUNTAIN, 6.2 *m.* A fire lookout stands on the summit.

Mounting by easy grades and wide curves the trail penetrates the high rocky shoulder (4,970 alt.), from which it descends into open country, scattered over with small forest growth. Below, to the east, flow the narrow waters of LADY CREEK (R) and the deep-gorged and more tumultuous ZIGZAG RIVER.

The route, again mounting, follows up the ridgeway between the upper Zigzag River (R) and LOST CREEK (L), both of which are formed by the melting snows of Zigzag Glacier. Mount Hood's white summit stands perpetually before the traveler's sight.

Entering the MOUNT HOOD PRIMITIVE AREA, 9.5 *m.*, the Zigzag Trail climbs into lovely PARADISE PARK, 10 *m.* (see *Paradise Park Trail*). The STADTER BURIED FOREST lies above on the mountain slope (*see sign*).

From Zigzag Mountain to Paradise Park this route is through

the Bull Run Reserve and must be traversed with the utmost care and regard for cleanliness and fire prevention. Secure fire permit before entering area. The trail is closed in seasons of extreme fire danger.

TOUR 5

Camp Creek Forest Camp—Still Creek Guard Station—Still Creek Forest Camp; 8.1 m., Still Creek Trail.

Still Creek Trail traverses a widely varying section that amply serves the pleasures of the hiker, equestrian, overnight camper, fisherman, and the student of plant and wild life. The major portion of the route parallels Still Creek and penetrates forested areas and open spaces. Good drinking water is plentiful along the way. Numerous clearings provide ample feeding grounds for saddle horses.

From CAMP CREEK CAMP, 0 *m.*, the trail climbs the forested grade southward, and FLAG MOUNTAIN SADDLE at 1.3 *m.* At 1.7 *m.* is a view (R) of a huge MONOLITH and the cliffs of HUNCHBACK MOUNTAIN to the south.

The route continues through forests of Douglas fir, western red cedar, hemlock, white pine, alder and maple interspersed with shrubs of elderberry, salmonberry, vine maple and salal. In the more open glades grow such flowers as bleeding heart, trillium, and lupine.

At 3 *m.* is a small stream (*good drinking water*) and the STILL CREEK GUARD STATION (*unoccupied, except in emergencies*). The trail then descends to the level of the creek and enters open country. Huckleberry, chinquapin, and rhododendron bushes border the trail. Indian paintbrush, tiger lilies, and star flowers are plentiful. Chipmunks are everywhere. As the route leaves the forests it leaves also the bird life. The varied thrush, blue jay, red-breasted nuthatch, and western wren prefer the more wooded areas.

Still Creek is forded at 4.5 *m.* and again 5.1 *m.* For the next mile the route traverses a barren, rocky slope. Visible to the north is Tom-Dick-Harry Mountain, to the northeast is Multorpor Hill, to the south is Eureka Peak, and to the southwest is Devil's Peak.

At 5.8 *m.* the trail enters the STILL CREEK PLANTING and proceeds through this young plantation of forest trees. Leaving the plantation at 6.8 *m.*, the Still Creek Trail crosses Still Creek, 6.9 *m.* Here the trail re-enters the old growth timber and continues to an intersection with the Shearer Burn Road at SUMMIT MEADOWS, 8.1 *m.* and the STILL CREEK FOREST CAMP.

TOUR 6

Twin Bridges—Paradise Park; 6 m., Paradise Park Trail.

This well-maintained, two-foot trail of easy grade mounts to the northeast from the TWIN BRIDGES FOREST CAMP on State 50, 0 *m.*, and for the first mile switches sharply back and forth along EAST ZIGZAG MOUNTAIN above the ZIGZAG RIVER (L). At 0.9 *m.* is a good view to the south of the mountains Tom-Dick-Harry, Hunchback, Flag, and Multorpor, and of the Loop Highway at the Laurel Hill turn.

At 1 *m.* the trail penetrates a closely forested area of second growth Douglas fir, western red cedar, western hemlock, western white pine, and mountain alder, with such shrubs as mountain ash, chinquapin, rhododendron, vine maple, and Oregon grape in frequent evidence. Flowers and herbs are Indian paintbrush, dwarf dogwood, Mount Hood lily, blue pentstemon, squaw grass, and many others.

At 2.3 *m.* Mount Hood comes to view. The trail, still following the north side of the Zigzag Canyon with the white ribbon of the river far below, climbs to a VIEWPOINT at 2.5 *m.*, from which the Little Zigzag Canyon can be seen to the east. The Paradise Trail crosses a blow-down area of old fires, 3.8 *m.*, and at 3.9 *m.* reaches a small creek (*drinking water*).

At 4 *m.* the trail enters a fine stand of mountain hemlock. At this altitude snow lies on the ground until late in the season, obscuring the trail, but is normally gone by July 15. Such wild flowers as wild heliotrope, lamb's-tongue, buttercups, and Indian paintbrush spring into brilliant bloom beside great banks of late-lingering snow.

PARADISE PARK, 6 *m.* (*stoves, shelter*), in the MOUNT HOOD PRIMITIVE AREA, is the most beautiful of the natural parks, or mountain meadows, in the entire Mount Hood area with the exception of the more remote Eden Park on the north side. These open areas are vividly colored with alpine blooms in mid or late summer intermingled with snowwhite heads of Indian basket grass, sheltering small blue anemones and delicate collensia. Blue huckleberry, black currant, and heather add a green touch, and dwarf hemlock, and scrub juniper sprawl along the ground. A few noble firs stand here. From the park's high points many mountain landmarks can be seen on clear days. To the south are Government Camp, Olallie Butte, and Mount Jefferson; to the east is Mount Hood; to the north are Larch Mountain, Lost Lake, HiYu Mountain, Mount St. Helens and Mount Rainier; and to the west are Devils Peak, Zigzag Mountain, Burnt Lake and, far distant Portland.

Along this trail and in the park the songs of birds are frequently heard. These are the varied thrush, Oregon jay, northern junco, western wren, warblers, red-breasted nuthatch, and Clark nutcracker. Pine squirrels and chipmunks are relatively common.

While camping with his parents in Paradise Park in August 1926, seven-year-old Jackie Strong became lost in the wild area to the west. After much wandering, during which he fed on huckleberries and raw trout, saw a cougar, and protected himself against each night's cold by a brush lean-to, he was found on the fourth day just below Yocum Ridge. His rescuers were three members of a mountaineering group called the Crag Rats. Two hundred men had taken to the field, including members of the Mazamas, the Trails Club, forty army infantrymen, Portland and state highway police and deputy sheriffs, and numerous individuals. The Forest Service had hurried food and supplies to the field camps. Not greatly frightened at his predicament, young Strong walked out unharmed and confident, incredulous at the great concern over him.

(Optional return routes: Timberline Trail to Timberline Lodge, 6 m., or Zigzag Mountain Way to Rhododendron, 10 m.).

TOUR 7

Barlow Forest Camp—Hidden Lake—Sand Canyon; 4.3 m, Hidden Lake Way.

One of the most scenic and interesting of the mountain byways is the trail that mounts from the Loop Highway

(State 50), at the BARLOW FOREST CAMP, 0 *m.*, and follows the ridgeway to the west of the deep, gravelly gorge of LITTLE ZIGZAG RIVER (L).

Bearing to the north and east, with the summit of the mountain lifting ahead and visible at almost every point, this trail climbs through young Douglas firs, spruces, and mountain hemlocks to a junction with the HIDDEN LAKE TRAIL, 2.1 *m.* (L), to HIDDEN LAKE, 1 *m.*

The ZIGZAG RIVER CANYON (R) deepens and narrows as the steep trail mounts. The grandeur of the gorge, the bold and impressive features of the mountain, and the sweeping vistas of the Cascades to the southeast compensate for the arduous ascent.

As the trail reaches and passes beyond the 4,000 foot altitude, the prevailing evergreens are of the subalpine type, such as silver fir, Engelmann spruce, mountain hemlock, red cedar, and white pine. Birds are not common in this area but rock rabbits are frequently seen.

At 2.6 *m.* the ascent becomes extremely steep in places but is eased somewhat by the conveniently laid trail. An occasional small mountain meadow emerges from the timber, which grows more open and scattered, principally in the watered terrains. Heather, Mount Hood lilies, and squaw grass grow on the more hospitable slopes. The long scar of SAND CANYON (R), beginning high above at timberline, continues down the mountain as a shallow creek.

The trail crosses the diminished stream of the Little Zigzag, 4.1 *m.*, more than a mile below the snout of PALMER GLACIER whose melting snows and ice form this stream. At 4.3 *m.* Sand Canyon is easily negotiable. The bold features of ILLUMINATION POINT and CRATER ROCK hang almost overhead, and the smoking west side fumaroles are visible. If it is clear and bright, the brilliance of the sun on the ice fields and the contrasting shadows of rocks and ice fissures afford a grand and awesome study.

TOUR 8

Junction State 50—Yocum Falls—Mirror Lake; 2.1 m., Yocum Falls—Mirror Lake Trail.

Mirror Lake Trail leaves the MOUNT HOOD LOOP HIGHWAY (State 50), 0 *m.*, at a point two miles west of

Government Camp, almost at the crest of LAUREL HILL. It climbs south over easy grades with YOCUM FALLS, 0.5 *m.* (R), far below.

The trail mounts the north slope of TOM-DICK-HARRY MOUNTAIN through cedars, firs, and hemlocks, and from the first bench, 1.2 *m.*, follows down the gentle west-turning slope to MIRROR LAKE, 2.1 *m.* The small but lovely lake gets its name from the fact that Mount Hood, standing to the north, reflects its majestic image on the water's mirror-like surface. Photographs and paintings of this scene are widely known.

TOUR 9

Government Camp—Camp Blossom; 4.5 m., Camp Blossom Trail.

Camp Blossom Trail is the original route to the summit of Mount Hood by those using Government Camp as a base. During the summer months, it is a scenic and enjoyable hiking and riding trail to and from Timberline Lodge. In the winter the route becomes the Blossom Ski Trail, a run of considerable difficulty open to experts only.

The first mile of the route northward from GOVERN-MENT CAMP, 0 *m.*, is through deep avenues of large Western hemlock and Sitka spruce, with a scattered profusion of the red-berried mountain ash. At 1.5 *m.* an alpine forest of balsam fir and mountain hemlock. At 3 *m.* the prevailing evergreens are the smaller subalpine firs and pines.

At 3.4 *m.* the trail turns (L) and follows up SAND CANYON to CAMP BLOSSOM, 4.5 *m.*

TOUR 10

Summit Ranger Station—Trillium Lake—Jackpot Meadows; 6.3 m. The Oregon Skyline (Pacific Crest) Trail.

From SUMMIT RANGER STATION, 0 *m.*, on the Mount Hood Loop Highway (State 50) the Oregon Skyline Trail leads southward around the east base of Multorpor Mountain through SWIM and SUMMIT MEADOWS (*see Hiking and Riding Tour No. 5*) to the south end of the Trillium Lake Recreational Project. Dropping down the ridge over easy grades and through small timber the trail enters a long meadow.

At 1.8 *m.* is TRILLIUM LAKE (R), formerly Mud Lake, and one of the sources of Mud Creek (L) which courses the meadow's length from north to south.

Winding along, now high above and again at the creek's edge, the trail continues steadily descending. As the valley broadens at 2.9 *m.* small mountain meadows, profusely covered with huckleberry growth, are divided and encircled by evergreens, many of them large spruces and hemlocks with a sprinkling of lodgepole pines, Douglas and balsam firs. An old burn, 3.5 *m.* slowly greening over, stretches to the right. Distant peaks appear to the south.

The trail follows the east bank of Mud Creek to its confluence with the SALMON RIVER, 5.3 *m.* At 6 *m.* the Trillium Lake Trail crosses the Linney Creek Road.

Right on this road to Linney Creek Guard Station (*see Hiking and Riding Tour No. 1*).

JACKPOT MEADOWS, 6.3 *m.,* lies in the heart of the Cascades and in one of the region's most scenic areas, now being developed by Forest Service.

This route is a part of the old Skyline (riding) Trail that continues south from Jackpot Meadows, following the crest of the Cascades to the California line. (*Inquire of forester before attempting the longer trail, which at several points offers an alternate choice of route. Unless the traveler is familiar with rough mountain travel and able to care for himself under conditions of hardships, he should not undertake this trip unaccompanied by a capable guide. Riding time, 30 days.*)

TOUR 11

Timberline Lodge—Paradise Park—Eden Park—Cloud Cap Inn—Timberline Lodge; 36.5 m., Timberline or "Round the Mountain" Trail.

This is Mount Hood's most scenic and most spectacular trail, sections of which have been developed for travel (*afoot or horseback*) only within the past two years. It encircles the white peak of Mount Hood just about timberline.

Leaving TIMBERLINE LODGE at the junction of the

Summit Trail, 0 *m.* (*see Climbing Routes to the Summit*), this major trail, sometimes called the "Hat Band," leads northwest across the glades and through scattered hemlocks and silver firs.

One hundred yards northwest of the west wing of Timberline Lodge lies the open air TIMBERLINE THEATER built in 1938. The amphitheater which seats about 500, extends approximately north and south, with the stage situated at the lower, southern end of a small natural bowl. A low wall of rubble masonry, complementing the architecture of the Lodge foundation, surrounds and outlines the amphitheater. The seats, massive, hand-hewn logs of Douglas fir arranged in a quarter circle, rise in tiers, following the natural contour of the mountain slope. A backdrop of wild mountain scenery gives epic connotations to the play and to the acting. No less than six major peaks of the Cascade chain are visible on clear days: Mount Jefferson, Olallie Butte, Mount Washington, Three-fingered Jack, Three Sisters, and Black Butte. Curtaining the bases of these white draped peaks is a saucer-like rim of nearer foothills, green-clad and many-mooded in summer, but snowy-immaculate in winter. On the stage of this amphitheater, in season, a varied program of appropriate theatrical entertainment is presented.

TIMBERLINE CABIN or CAMP BLOSSOM, 0.6 *m.* (*for use by mountain climbers*), stands in protective timber on the east edge of SAND CANYON, 0.7 *m.* At 0.9 *m.*, LITTLE ZIGZAG CANYON is crossed.

Threading the timbered heights, the route climbs past several springs and to impressive viewpoints from which the peak above and the surrounding country are visible.

At 2.1 *m.* the way descends into the ZIGZAG CANYON, a wide glacial wash; numerous small streams feed the waters of the melting upper snows into the ZIGZAG RIVER. The crest of the opposite ridge is reached at 3.9 *m.* Here the MOUNT HOOD PRIMITIVE AREA is entered.

At 4.5 *m.* is the junction with the Paradise Park Trail (*see Paradise Park Trail*). Crossing LOST CREEK, 4.6 *m.*, a branch of the Sandy River, the route enters beautiful PARADISE PARK, 4.7 *m.* (*stone shelter, horsefeed*). This is one of the loveliest of all Mount Hood meadows, richly carpeted with flowers in season and frequently visited by hikers. Of recent years, in winter, it has become popular with the more ardent and skilled skiers. Snowshoe rabbits are abundant. An excellent view of Mount Hood's white cap is presented as the trail leaves the park.

SLIDE MOUNTAIN, 5.3 *m.*, stands L. as the trail traverses the open ridge and descends into the upper SANDY RIVER GORGE, 6 *m.*, the deepest gorge in the entire Mount Hood area. At 6.7 *m.* and 7.1 *m.* two viewpoints offer excellent scenic studies of Sandy and Reid Glaciers (R) and of several small waterfalls.

At 8.9 *m.* the SANDY RIVER is crossed. The Muddy Forks Trail, 9.2 *m.* (L), is closed to travel, to protect the Bull Run Reserve. The Upper Sandy forest guard stands at this point.

The trail now proceeds to RAMONA FALLS, 9.6 *m.* (*shelter*). Within the next mile two creeks are forded and at 11.2 *m.* is the first of several campsites marking the scenes of recent activity in trail building (*spring water*).

The ascent to Bald Mountain Ridge, 11.3 *m.*, is an arduous but scenic stretch of the trail. At the rockslide, 12.2 *m.*, is a viewpoint with a spring just beyond, at 12.3 *m.* The summit of BALD MOUNTAIN RIDGE, 12.7 *m.* (4,400 alt.), is one of the highest points on the trail; with a short side route (R) to the top of Bald Mountain, leading also to the emergency LOOKOUT STATION. (*Campsite at trail junction; water 200 yards L.*)

The Timberline Trail at this point curves gradually to the northeast and east. At 13.9 *m.* the Lost Lake trail (*see Hiking and Riding Tour No. 15*) leads left. Still on Bald Mountain Ridge, 14.3 *m.*, a superb view of the Upper Muddy Fork of the Sandy River, the glaciers and the mountain's northwest snowslope is presented.

A second trail construction campsite, 15.5 *m.* (L), affords water and horsefeed. Beyond this point several small creeks are forded and at 16.3 *m.* CATHEDRAL RIDGE (6,935 alt.) is crossed.

The CAIRN BASIN, 16.8 *m.* (*stone shelter, water and horsefeed, R. 200 feet*) opens out into EDEN PARK, most beautiful of all the mountain meadows.

In this region wild flowers burst into bloom each summer, almost at the edge of the retreating snows. It has been said by an authoritative botanist, that there are more varieties of alpine flowers in this area than in any other place in the world. Flowers (*do not gather*) generally bloom in abundance from early in July and through the first week of August. There is also a brief riot of color along this trail in early fall when the vegetation is first touched by frost. Game is common; elk, deer and bear are occasionally seen.

Leaving Eden Park, the route three times crosses the headwaters of LADD CREEK. These high mountain streams are crystal clear in the early morning but on summer afternoons, under the melting warmth of the sun which slowly dissolves the glacial snow, become small roaring torrents of milky water. At this altitude north slopes are the most deeply wooded on the mountain, with lodgepole pine a common variety.

The headwaters of CLEAR CREEK gather in the wooded WY'EAST BASIN, 18.1 *m.* (*horsefeed*). DOLLAR LAKE lies a quarter-mile to the L. at 18.6 *m.* ELK COVE, 19.6 *m.* (*stone shelter, horsefeed*), stands on the banks of ELK CREEK.

COE CREEK is crossed, 20.1 *m.*, and the west and east branches of narrow COMPASS CREEK, 21 *m.*, with its cascades and waterfalls. ELIOT CREEK, 22.9 *m.*, courses through the alpine forests from the glacier above. At this point the route leaves the MOUNT HOOD PRIMITIVE AREA.

CLOUD CAP INN, 23.1 *m.* (*R. 300 feet*), amidst scattered alpine growth and open glades, is the well-known north side resort (*see Motor Tour 2*). Mount Adams and Mount Rainier loom magnificently to the north.

At the TILLY JANE FOREST CAMP and GUARD STATION, 23.8 *m.*, is (L) the HOOD RIVER AMERICAN LEGION CAMP (*shelter, water*), also (L) is the road that winds through balsam timber down to the Mount Hood Loop Highway (*see Motor Tour 2*).

Just beyond POLALLY CREEK CANYON, 24 *m.* (L), is the junction (R) with the Cooper Spur Trail, 24.7 *m.*, to the white crest above (*see Climbing Routes to the Summit*).

A fine view of the peak and ELIOT GLACIER appears (R) at 25 *m.*, and another of LAMBERSON BUTTE SPUR ahead and to the left. The snowfield of NEWTON CLARK GLACIER gleams above at 26.6 *m.* as the mounting trail crosses LAMBERSON BUTTE (6,700 alt.). At the Butte's Crest, GNARL RIDGE, 27 *m.* (*stone shelter, water 300 feet*), affords a fine example of the struggle of trees at timberline. Horsefeed is obtainable at 27.6 *m.*

NEWTON CREEK, 29.3 *m.* (*campsite, water*), a stream of melted snow, tumbles down from Newton Clark Glacier.

The Timberline Trail now curves gradually to the southwest where it crosses CLARK CREEK, 30.5 *m.* PENCIL FALLS, 30.7 *m.*, on a branch of Heather Creek, comes into view. Good shaded campsites (*horsefeed*) are available at 31.1 *m.* and 32.1 *m.* At 32.7 *m.* is a side trail.

Left on this trail to HOOD RIVER MEADOWS (*see Motor Tour 2*), which sweeps down the east slope to the Loop Highway. UMBRELLA FALLS, 1 *m.*, on this side route is made by the cascading waters of the EAST FORK OF THE HOOD RIVER.

Crooking around the south side of the mountain over a broken terrain, the trail turns directly west and crosses the glaciated wash of WHITE RIVER, 34.3 *m.*, at this altitude, a narrow chalky stream. At 36 *m.* is the MIDDLE FORK OF THE SALMON RIVER.

The trail arcs to the southwest and descends through silver firs to its point of origin just west of TIMBERLINE LODGE, 36.5 *m.*

TOUR 12

Barlow Pass—Butte Springs—Blue Box Summit; 11 m. Barlow Ridge Trail.

From the Mount Hood Loop Highway (State 35) at BARLOW PASS, 0 *m.*, the Ridge Trail winds due east, down the beautiful WHITE RIVER CANYON through tall Balsam firs and mountain hemlocks. At times it follows almost at the stream's edge and again high above. Turning southeast it rounds the east shoulder of BARLOW BUTTE, 1 *m.* (5,035 alt.). In DEVILS HALF ACRE, 1.6 *m.*, a marshy meadow in midsummer beautiful with alpine flowers, there are a number of beaver dams—one of the few remaining areas in the state where the industrial handiwork of these nearly extinct water animals can be studied. A deforested burn extends for some distance southward.

The trail, high on the ridgeway that divides the White River (L) from Barlow Creek (R), follows south through a patch of small Douglas firs. At 3.6 *m.* it rounds to the east of BARLOW BUTTE (5,158 alt.), and penetrates the deep, silent forests of hemlock, larch, and spruce, scattered through with an occasional lodgepole pine. The Balsam firs—noble, silver, and white—comprise over 50 per cent of the trees in this area on the east slope of the Cascades.

The noisy sound of White River's brawling waters is distinguishable (L) at 4.7 m. Dropping down to the OLD BARLOW ROAD, 5.4 m., the trail follows into the deep timber.

The course is now southwest. At 6 m. BARLOW CREEK is crossed. The climbing trail follows the south slopes of FROG LAKE BUTTE, its summit topped by a Fire Lookout station glimpsed through the firs (R). The trail, reaching its highest point, 7.2 m., drops down into the creek-bed of GREEN LAKE CREEK, 7.9 m.

BUTTE SPRINGS, 8.6 m., is the source of one of the region's numerous creeks.

Barlow Ridge Trail, swinging south through a region of wild game and great isolation, crosses FROG CREEK at 10.3 m. and at 10.6 m. reaches the Abbott Road. Turning north along this rutted roadway, now seldom used, the route soon intersects with the Wapinitia Highway (State 50), 11 m., just south of the BLUE BOX SUMMIT.

TOUR 13

Hood River Meadows—Elk Meadows—Junction Cooper Spur Road; 10 m. Hood River Meadows—Cold Springs Creek Trail.

This trail intersects with the Mount Hood Loop Highway (State 35) at HOOD RIVER MEADOWS FOREST CAMP, 0 m., two miles north of Bennett Pass. From this grassy area of wide perspectives, on the lower east slope of the mountain, the trail rises sharply. Crossing CLARK CREEK, 1 m., it mounts to the ridge crest, 2 m., which it descends rapidly to NEWTON CREEK, 2.5 m. ELK MOUNTAIN (5,681 alt.) lifts immediately to the east.

The trail, climbing from the deeply wooded creek bed, enters beautiful ELK MEADOWS, 3.5 m., an area of luxuriant growth that once was a favorite feeding ground of the elk, formerly native here in great numbers. To the east the timbered benches fall away into flat meadow land, while to the west, mounting above timberline, is Mount Hood's white summit.

Leaving Elk Meadows, in summer rich with alpine bloom

and visited by the songbirds of high altitudes, the trail winds northward along Cold Springs Creek to a junction with the COOPER SPUR ROAD at HOMESTEAD INN, 10 *m.* (*see Motor Tour 2*).

TOUR 14

Robin Hood Forest Camp—Gumjuwac Saddle—Badger Lake; 5.5 m., Badger Lake Trail.

From the ROBIN HOOD FOREST CAMP and RANGER STATION on (State 35), 0 *m.*, this trail climbs due east by a series of right and left turns to GUMJUWAC SADDLE, 2.5 *m.* The climb is steep, through broken terrain and small forest growth with scattered huckleberry, wild lilac, and fern.

Turning almost due south at the saddle or pass, the trail follows along the ridgeway. It rounds the crest of GUNSIGHT BUTTE, 3.5 *m.* (L), and drops down a long slope to the evergreen wooded shores of BADGER LAKE, 5.5 *m.* (4,436 alt.). This lovely mountain gem nestles at the foot (L) of BADGER BUTTE (5,992 alt.). The BADGER LAKE FOREST CAMP (*shelter, guard station*) makes this an ideal vacation site (*see Motor Tour 8*).

TOUR 15

Bald Mountain—Lolo Pass—Lost Lake—Wahtum Lake—Eagle Creek Forest Camp; 19.5 m. The Oregon Skyline (Lost Lake) Trail—Eagle Creek Trail.

This trail diverges northward from the Timberline Trail at a point just west of EDEN PARK, 0 *m.*, and comes down the precipitate and narrow ELK CREEK. Forests in this region are dense with scattered, small open areas, luxuriant with wild growth following the late melting snows.

At 3.1 *m.* the trail climbs through the timber just below historic LOLO PASS (L), and proceeds north over the old WALK UP TRAIL used for centuries by the Indian tribes as the principal route over the northern Cascades. Except for the few briefly lingering birds and the occasional cries of the marmot, martin, and lynx, this is a region of great stillness. Deer are commonly seen, bears amble out of hibernation to feast on the wild fruit, and eagles lift from the crags.

Skirting the shoulder of HIYU MOUNTAIN, 3.7 *m.*, the trail leaves Elk Creek. Climbing over the dividing ridge and the shoulder of SENTINEL PEAK, 4.8 *m.* (4,560 alt.), it proceeds northwest up JONES CREEK, 5.2 *m.* Both of these streams empty into the west fork of Hood River one mile east.

At 5.6 *m.* the trail crosses and climbs the creek bed around LOST LAKE BUTTE (R) to the forested level of LOST LAKE, 8 *m.* (3,140 alt.). This lake (227 acres), the most beautiful and remote of all lakes in the Mount Hood Recreation Area, has long been second only to the peak itself as a destination for the mountain lover. The reflection of the peak, seen from the north shore, is enchanting and unforgettable. Many pictures of the scene have been painted. As no glacial waters enter the lake, its summer temperature is suitable for swimming. The Lost Lake Guard Station is open in the summer months and many excellent and scenic trails, maintained by the Forest Service, radiate from the lake to alpine meadows and vista points. (*Camp ground, cabins, and good hiking.*)

CAMP CHINIDERE is on the shores of beautiful WAHTUM LAKE, 19.5 *m.* (*free public camp grounds; two shelters*). This lake, a half mile long and not quite so wide, is situated in a region of luxuriant forest growths. In the camp area, three signboards read: Herman Creek Trail (East); Eagle Creek Trail (West); Lost Lake Trail (South).

Ascent of the Peak

WHEN David Douglas visited the Columbia River Valley in 1825, it was his opinion that Mount Hood could not be scaled. He noted in his *Journal:* "In June I was within a few miles of Mount Hood. Its appearance presented barriers that could not be surmounted by any person to reach its summit." Nevertheless, eight years afterward he attempted the climb without, however, leaving any record of achieving the crest.

After him in 1845 Joel Palmer, later Oregon's superintendent of Indian Affairs, climbed a considerable distance up the glaciated valley of White River while seeking a route for the Barlow and Palmer wagon trains. Following an Indian trail in a northerly direction, together with Barlow and Lock, he turned from the trail at a point just east of present-day Timberline Lodge, and proceeded westward around the mountain to a deep canyon, probably Zigzag River. He camped, it is believed, in Paradise Park just below Mississippi Head. From this base on October 12 Palmer started up the ice and lava slopes, leaving his laggard companions. It is possible that he ascended to Illumination Rock, or high up on Triangle Moraine a mile above timberline. From this elevation he determined the route the wagon train should follow westward. For the next decade Palmer's account of his climbing exploit influenced all others attempting the journey; his route was the one generally followed, a section of it becoming the present well-known South Side Climb. Palmer Glacier, which he traversed, was named for him.

In 1854 Thomas J. Dryer, editor of the Portland *Oregonian,* claimed to have been the first to climb to the top of the peak, but his chronicle of the trip carried no identifying evidence of his actually having reached the summit. He apparently attained only the crest of Steel Cliff.

Not until July 11, 1857, is it certain that the pinnacle of Mount Hood was reached by white men. On that day four men, Henry L. Pittock, also of the *Oregonian,* the Reverend T. A. Woods, Lyman Chittenden, and Wilbur Cornell flung an American flag to the crest breezes. The four then formed a circle around the flag and gave three cheers. The climb from Summit Meadows consumed seven and one-half hours, and was spectacular in the last stretches because they were without a guiding precedent. They had only their boots and climbing "staves" to assist them. Their unprotected hands and faces were severely scorched and they suffered excruciating pain for days thereafter.

The first women to climb to the summit were Miss Mary Robinson and Miss Fanny Case. They climbed together with several male companions, in the summer of 1867.

The first guide to the mountain was Perry Vickers who settled at Summit Meadows in 1868. Later came Cornelius Gray, who likewise built a cabin for travelers and became a peak guide. Indeed, all early residents in this section were trail guides and "white peak men," notably Oliver C. Yocum, the pioneer settler at Government Camp and a tireless climber, William G. Steel, who lingered here, homesteading, and Francis E. Little.

As late as 1865 Mount Hood, from time to time as of old, provided its own illumination. Pioneers of the region mention several occasions when "an intermittent column of fire issued from the crater," and the mountain was "enveloped in smoke and flames." But these were the last eruptions of a dying volcano.

On July 4, 1870, Perry Vickers climbed the eroded lava slopes to the high western ridges and the summit. Here he built a huge bonfire, providing the mountain with its first artificial illumination. No one saw this puny attempt; all being engrossed in their own displays of fireworks.

Three years later Vickers offered his services to Portland's Fourth of July "Celebration Committee" for another attempt at illuminating the mountain. The committee turned down the offer chiefly on the grounds that it would be too expensive, but partly because they believed no man could live in the raw night air of the summit. To disprove this contention Vickers climbed the mountain alone, spent the night there, and set off ten displays of fire for the benefit of "a committee of twenty-five persons of unimpeachable veracity." By this exploit Vickers became the first person to spend the night atop Mount Hood.

In 1877 a party from The Dalles made an unsuccessful attempt to light the mountain. It was their plan to illuminate the north side, which would not have been visible from Portland. In 1885 a Portland group with a plentiful supply of red fire and a clockwork ignition system made another attempt. After tedious hours of climbing and setting up the display, a falling rock set off the "infernal machine" prematurely, in the middle of the afternoon.

July 4, 1887, saw the white crest for the first time successfully and brilliantly illuminated. Under the leadership of Will Steel, a party of seven transported 100 pounds of red fire up the steep slopes. The spot selected for the display was at the base of what thereafter was called Illumination Rock. Most of the party returned to camp, leaving two of its members, Dr. Keene and Steel, to spend several chilly hours until darkness. At half-past nine Keene and Steel rejoiced at being able to see the glow from fireworks displays in Portland, Vancouver, and Prineville. They realized, then, that their flares would be visible also. Promptly at half-past eleven, the hour agreed upon, the display was lighted. It lasted for fifty-eight seconds and was a complete success, being seen over a wide area of eastern and western Oregon and southern Washington. The local press of several communities commented on it as "the most unique event of the day."

Gradually the south slope area became known as the "starting point for climbs to the summit." The first climbing clubs were organized and their members, with increasing frequency, visited the white upper reaches. Each year a larger number ascended to the crest until the yearly count surpassed the thousand mark. Under the stimulating influence of the Oregon Alpine Club, organized in 1887, peak climbing became Oregon's supreme sporting achievement. Guides became many and proficient.

On the north side, the first ascent to the summit was by Newton Clark, for whom the glacier was then named. A homesteader near the town of Hood River, Clark was a civil engineer. He explored many of the mountain slopes that previously were believed unscalable by man. On August 11, 1887, with William J. Smith and Elmer Rand, Clark traversed Eliot Glacier, over Coe Glacier above Barrett Spur, to Pulpit

Rock, and on to Cathedral Ridge, along which they proceeded to the top.

Will and Douglas Langille of Cloud Cap Inn were the first to ascend by the Cooper Spur Route, in 1893, but both had been climbing over Newton Clark Glacier since 1889. However, it was Dave Cooper who first became a regular guide over the Spur.

When the Mazamas were organized on July 19, 1894, on the summit of Mount Hood, membership in the club was conditioned on the applicant's having previously climbed to the summit of at least one snow peak on which there is a living glacier and which can be reached only on foot. The name "Mazama" was adopted from that most agile of climbers of western peaks, the mountain goat. Their slogan, "Nesika Klatawa Sahle," in Chinook jargon means "We climb high." On this occasion Douglas Langille guided the climbers over the northeast shoulder of the peak. By 1897 Langille had made fifty ascents over Cooper Spur, sometimes using the trail now known as the Sunshine Route, which the Langille brothers developed.

Two accidents, one of them fatal, occurred on the white slopes in the nineties. Late in August, 1896, near the big crevasse on the south side, the three daughters of William Killingsworth of Portland were descending the mountain, having climbed to the summit. An explosion was heard and looking up they saw a huge boulder fall from the crater wall and come hurtling down the snowfield toward them. One of the girls, Fay Killingsworth, was directly in its course. Instead of hitting her, however, it bounded completely over her, but threw up such a mass of snow that the girl was swept bodily into a crevasse fifty feet beyond. Fortunately she was soon rescued unharmed by another party member, Frank N. Spicer. The second accident was on July 11, 1897. Late the previous afternoon Frederic Kern, a sixty-year-old Swiss grocer of Portland, registered at Cloud Cap Inn. Walking the distance from Hood River to the mountain, he inquired of Will Langille of the routes to the summit, said he had climbed in his youth in Switzerland and was interested in the volcanic features of the peak. The following morning at 4 o'clock, refusing companionship, he set out alone over Eliot Glacier. When far up on the moraine he left the "route," veering to the southeast where he passed from the sight of Mrs. James L. Langille, mother of the Langille brothers, who was watching with field glass from the Inn. How Kern met his death after that was never accurately known. When he did not return by half-past five Will Langille set out to find him. Night fell, but under the half light of the moon the searcher found Kern's body lying on the icy slopes of Newton Clark glacier, where it had been carried over the brow of the sharp bluff above. Apparently he had been struck by a shower of rocks and dashed to his death.

After 1900 summer ascents of Mount Hood became frequent, so much so as to make itemized chronicling almost impossible for the historian. Climbing had become so popular by 1915 that Lije Coalman was hired by the Forest Service to erect a shelter cabin and fire lookout on the tip of the peak. At the edge of the timber midway between the crest and Government Camp, Timberline Cabin or Camp Blossom was constructed as a base of supplies and a way station for climbers.

Sometimes spoken of as the "man of the mountain," Lije Coalman, making his first climb with Yocum in 1897, was for thirty-one years Mount Hood's best loved character and most popular guide. Well over six feet in height, he was openhearted, read Emerson's essays from a well-worn volume he carried, and as a pastime frequently indulged in uncommon and difficult mathematical problems. Coalman often rescued incautious adventurers who had become lost on the snowfields.

The Mazama record book at the Lookout Cabin holds the names of the first individuals to complete the ascent in the winter. Lije Coalman and Charles E. Warner broke all American records for winter ascents of glacial peaks, when on March 8, 1915, they mounted to the crest. On December 31, 1915, Warner and W. W. Evans climbed from Cloud Cap Inn, encountering two snow storms. They spent the night in the Lookout Cabin, then made their way down the south side to Government Camp. Again on January 1, 1920, Warner and Clem Blakney left Camp Blossom at 4:30 a.m. and reached the summit at 1:10 p.m. Returning, they reached Government Camp at 6:40 p.m. Except for the constant probability of severe storm and the penetrating temperature of the high altitude, winter climbing has advantages not equalled in summer, principally because of tramping over well-packed snow.

Since the death of Kern in 1897 five people have lost their lives. Nearly all accidents on the peak have resulted from taking chances or from carelessness. In 1916 while attempting to climb by the south side route, Mr. and Mrs. A. H. Edlefsen, unsuitably garbed in street clothes and unequipped, became wearied upon reaching Crater Rock. Disregarding Coalman's admonition that they remain there until the ascending party returned, they began the descent alone. When part way down they abandoned the sure course for a shorter one, and became lost in the timber with fog rolling up the mountainside. Darkness fell and with it came a storm of rain, sleet, and snow. Sustaining themselves on huckleberries, which were ripe, they had spent two days in the high forest when discovered not far from Zigzag canyon, two miles from Government Camp Hotel.

On the north side in the 1920's a second timberline shelter was built by the Hood River Post of the American Legion, as a "family camp" for the 200 or more persons who make the Legion's annual climb to the summit. From this opening in the forests that fringe Tilly Jane Creek, the largest yearly supervised climbs of any snow peak in the Pacific Northwest were launched in 1921. "Fathered" by Kent Shoemaker, these ascents have usually been led by members of the Hood River Crag Rats, a mountaineering group organized in 1926. Only in one instance have these climbs been exceeded in the number of those participating—the ascent made by the Mantle Club of Portland, in 1936, which numbered 411 men and women.

Each new year the thrill of being the first to reach the summit has drawn a few adventurous climbers up the winter-whitened slopes. More than a score have achieved this record. On New Year's Day, 1926, two grown youths, Leslie Brownlee and Al Feyerabend, fully equipped, unsuccessfully attempted this feat. Climbing through snow flurries above Camp Blossom, at an early morning hour they advanced up the moraine of White River glacier. Overtaken at Crater Rock by zero visibility, Brownlee, who became exhausted, gave up and began to retrace his steps to the highway, far below. Battling the wind and snow which roared across the high wastes, Feyerabend sought to continue the climb alone. When

TIMBERLINE LODGE

MAZAMA LODGE

Monn

Atkeson

SUNRISE

MAIN LOUNGE
TIMBERLINE LODGE

NORTH WINOWS
TIMBERLINE LODGE

Atkeson

**TYPICAL BEDROOM,
TIMBERLINE LODGE**

**STAIRWAY, TIMBERLINE
LODGE**

THE EXPERT

TOBOGGANING

U. S. Forest Ser

The Oregonian

SKI TOURNAMEN

CREVASSES

CLIMBING THE SERACS,
UPPER ICE FALLS OF
ELIOT GLACIER

ZIGZAG GLACIER PRONG OF SANDY RIVER

this proved futile he too began the return journey. The two were now completely separated and soon both were lost. Apparently Feyerabend's keener cunning and a rift in the storm led him on a course that brought him back to the shelter at Camp Blossom. Leslie Brownlee, despite a search that lasted for eight days and enlisted scores of searchers, including trained mountaineers, army men, and forest rangers, was never found.

Because of the greatly increased sports patronage in recent years more mishaps have occurred. While climbing steep snow over Cooper Spur on Sunday morning, July 17, 1927, part of a Mazama squad broke loose from the tie line and sped rapidly toward a crevasse 100 feet deep. Only the swiftness of their involuntary glissade saved them from worse tragedy than they suffered; they completely breached the chasm and after falling twenty feet were deposited on the far lip of the crevasse. In this accident the body of Dr. Stanton W. Stryker was pierced through with an alpenstock. Others were injured. Somewhat disregardful of normal precautions, three youths climbed above the Big Crevasse on July 5, 1932, before the life-line had been anchored for the summer. All were unroped and carried only alpenstocks. Glen Gullickson slipped and sped downward to his death on the exposed rocks. While a party was crossing a blind crevasse at the head of Coe Glacier on Labor Day, 1933, the roof collapsed and three members fell below the surface, sawing off the tie rope on the rough ice-edge. Of the three who fell into the crevasse, Miss Esther Gilman was seriously injured. A roaring gale was blowing and since the mishap had occurred only a half-mile from the summit, with night falling, security for the party lay only in the cabin above. Up the long snow-covered area, aided by a rope line hastily let down the course, the girl was carried. There the group of thirteen remained for two days, descending by the safer south side route. Carried and at times slid over the upper reaches, Miss Gilman was placed on the toboggan cached at Crater Rock by the Wy'east Climbers, and the down-trip to Government Camp completed.

Few in number but exacting in requirements for membership, the Wy'east Climbers were organized in December, 1930. Mountaineers of proven ability, these men have frequently led climbing parties and rescue groups and have provided first aid for injured climbers and skiers. But the best peak men may encounter trouble. Two Wy'easters, Ralph Calkin and Henry Corbett, accompanied by Elsie Hall and Jean Blake, rode an avalanche over the northern wall of Cooper Spur onto Eliot Glacier in June 1937. While descending by the Sunshine route eighteen inches of newly-fallen snow began moving from under their feet. Despite all efforts to break their descent they were swept over the brink of the upper snowfield, dropping seventy-five feet. Only the cushioning mass of snow into which they fell saved them from possible death. Three of them suffered severe friction burns.

The mountain's most recent tragedy was on March 27, 1938. A winter climbing party of fourteen, forced back by blizzard when within a few hundred feet of the crest, was making its way toward Lone Fir Cabin when Roy Varney, a Mazaman, was overcome by exertion and chill. Forty-nine years old and at the time physically unequal to the feat of climbing, he died in the snow a short distance above the cabin. Meanwhile a fellow climber, Russell Gueffroy, twenty-nine and a Trails Club member, plunging on through the storm alone, presumably toward Camp Blossom, became lost in the timber of Sand Canyon. His frozen body, snow-covered, was found four days later. However, in view of the fact that thousands of people make the climb each year accidents and tragedies have been few.

Since 1932 a number of new summit routes have been followed out by adventurous mountaineers, particularly by members of the Mazamas and the Wy'east Climbers. Some of these are considered "stunt" climbs and are not for the inexperienced. A few vary the routes previously taken. Also, winter erosion, from time to time, alters the accessibility of old routes.

Today there are eleven routes to the crest of Mount Hood. Three of these are well-known and conventionally used by the majority of summit climbers; with the South Side Climb, beginning at Timberline Lodge, the safest and the one most frequently taken.

Mount Hood is America's most climbed major peak, an average of 1,500 persons ascending its rugged slopes each year. The annual "mass" climbs of the Mazamas and Hood River Legionnaires are supplemented by the numerous small parties that mount ant-like to the crest. Confirmed mountaineers make the journey several times a year, a few have climbed every month in a single year.

VIEW FROM THE SUMMIT

THE most magnificent view that Oregon affords awaits the climber from the summit of Mount Hood. Of the great snow sentinels of the Pacific Northwest, the third in rank, it rises above the common Cascadian elevation about 6,000 feet. Visible to the west on either side of the thread-like river, the Willamette Valley sweeps to the gray horizon of the Coast Range, 82 miles distant. The Pacific Ocean, because of the obstructing mountains, is not visible.

To the south stands the snow-covered, chimney-like top of Mount Jefferson in the backbone of the Cascades. Beyond lift the Three Sisters, white clad and remote, with the blue-green blur of Diamond Peak far against the southern skyline.

Eastward lies central and eastern Oregon, a widespread checkerboard of wheat and alfalfa fields, and sheep and cattle ranges, with the occasional deep-carved river canyon, "jagged as lightning down the colored miles." In the dim distance, the Blue Mountains, justifying their name, draw a turquoise blur along the receding earth-line. Sun will sometimes be seen shining over the intervening high desert area, while western Oregon lies wrapped in mists and cloud.

Beyond the deep and austere gorge of the Columbia River, stretching from east to west in the immediate northern foreground, rise the white peaks of the State of Washington. Slightly to the right is rugged Mount Adams, due north and farthest removed is Mount Rainier, while Mount St. Helens, a perfect white cone, lifts to the left of this sweeping panorama, serrated with other lesser and green-forested peaks. Like the mountain range area to the south, this northern green land is scattered with silver, gem-like lakes. Nearest of all, between the Columbia and the peak itself, lie the reflecting, placid surfaces of Lost Lake and Bull Run Lake, visibly the largest of all.

At the immediate feet of the climber spread Mount Hood's ten glaciers, blinding white in clear sun. From the snouts of these ancient ice masses more than a dozen rivers and creeks stream down the eroded lava and forest-clad slopes. Lower still, the highway girdle loops and turns through the flowering meadows and the evergreens of the Cascades, falling away to the state's agricultural levels, and its towns and villages— the homes of its nature lovers and recreationists, hundreds of whom each year climb Mount Hood to obtain this unmatchable view.

SUMMIT CLIMBS

Special Information: Latest information on climbing conditions should be obtained from Forest Service officials or experienced guides since at certain times summit routes are extremely unsafe.

Climbing conditions on Mount Hood change constantly: sun warmth, winds, storms, time of year and time of day, all, while varying the atmospheric appeal affect the security of footing. May and June are considered the safest months for climbing. The start should be made in the very early morning hours, preferably by daybreak. The warm afternoon hours should be avoided as hazardous. Because of repeated thawing and freezing the high talus slopes and ledges are definitely insecure in late summer.

Rock climbing and snow climbing require different skills, equipment suitable for the conditions, and an unrelaxed diligence to avoid accidents. Wear windproof clothing. Equipment should include alpenstock, heavy shoes, crampons, colored glasses, sunburn lotion, canteen, and flashlight. Leaders and qualified assistants should carry ice axes for cutting foot and handholds in snow and rock. One or more tie ropes should be carried by each party.

Climbers should be in prime physical condition when attempting this arduous pleasure. For one to become exhausted or unable to continue the upward journey hinders the entire party. Never climb the peak alone. It is always advisable to climb in company with one or more persons familiar with the route. In danger zones wise climbers go roped three and four together, thus enabling them to pull one another out of difficulty should accident occur. *Confidence should never overrule good judgment and ability.* "Stunt" climbing is inadvisable. By far the majority of professional and amateur climbers are conservative, seeking their own safety and that of others. *Do not take chances.*

Always seek shelter at the first threat of storm, which may strike suddenly and with blizzard intensity. If lost where fuel is available build a fire for warmth; its smoke will also serve as a signal for searchers. If near a snowfield, climb to its open reaches where you may be sighted by a searcher's fieldglass.

ROUTE 1

Timberline Lodge—Lone Fir Lookout—Palmer Glacier—Crater Rock—"The Chute"—Summit; 3.7 m., South Side Climb.

Safest and most popular route; time, 8 hours.

From a starting point just west of TIMBERLINE LODGE, 0 *m.*, this historic route of the earliest peak climbers proceeds along the Salmon River Canyon Ridge, over a well-defined trail to LONE FIR LOOKOUT (6,700 alt.), 0.8 *m.* (*summer fire lookout station*). Continuing due north the route crosses PALMER GLACIER, 1.5 *m.* (7,500 alt.). This active ice field, a half-mile wide, rather flat and devoid of crevasses owing to its smoothness and ease of travel, affords a minimum of hazard for the climber. White River lies in a canyon to the east. To the west is Zigzag Glacier, source of the Zigzag River which flows southwest and west into the Sandy River.

TRIANGULAR MORAINE, 2 *m.* (8,000 alt.), is a high rib of rock along the west rim of White River Glacier, left by early ice flows as they moved down the face of the mountain. WHITE RIVER GLACIER flows down the steep gorge (R), while far below the river's pumice-whitened waters emerge from the blue-green glacial ice.

MAKE-UP ROCK, 2.5 *m.* (9,500 alt.), at the north head of Triangular Moraine, rises above the great snow plain, and gets its name from the habit of climbers who here grease their faces and don dark glasses as protection from wind and snow burn. It is sometimes called Pack Rock.

Climbing an average of more than a thousand feet each half mile, the route crosses crevasse-furrowed snow and curves around wind-scourged crags to the base of CRATER ROCK, 3.1 *m.* (10,000 alt.). At the foot of this massive boulder a first aid toboggan, provided by the Wy'east Climbers, is kept for emergencies.

The route, on leaving Triangular Moraine, goes around the east side of Crater Rock, past the DEVIL's KITCHEN, 3.2 *m.* (10,400 alt.), a bare spot at the head of White River Glacier where numerous gas vents, or fumaroles, send forth from the mountain's dying internal fire sulphuric smudges. STEEL CLIFF (R) is a great wall of lava, named for William G. Steel, a pioneer in Mount Hood's recreational development. The cliff extends in broken ramparts to the summit of the peak, rising nearly a thousand feet above its southern base at the Kitchen (*see climbs 4 and 9*).

From the Devil's Kitchen the route angles westerly, up and over the HOGBACK, a high ridge of snow, to the HOT ROCKS, 3.3 *m.* (10,000 alt.), lying immediately below the "CHUTE," and some 50 yards north of the huge ever-steaming fumarole in Crater Rock. The gas vents in both the Devil's Kitchen and the Hot Rocks have shown temperatures of 193° F. Gasses from these fumaroles are deadly and have claimed one life. Victor F. Von Norman, a young University of Washington student, on August 27, 1934, was tempted to descend into one of the largest of these fumaroles. He was overcome almost immediately by the noxious gas, so dense as to exclude all oxygen from the atmosphere of the cavern. Of those who went to the victim's rescue, nine were seriously affected and two were rendered unconscious. Only when oxygen helmets were used, were recovery efforts successful, too late to save Von Norman's life.

Stretching up the "Chute" in summer are a series of ropes totaling 1,000 feet in length, anchored to iron pipes driven into the ice. These afford support for the climber up this steep grade which averages more than 30 degrees.

The CREST at the upper end of the "Chute," 3.6 *m.* (11,220 alt.), commands the most spectacular view of the entire climb. Below the sharp, 3,000-foot precipice of the north side hang the ice falls of COE and LADD GLACIERS, with their white fields spreading down the precipitous slopes to timberline.

At this point the route turns eastward, following the ridge for nearly 400 feet, to the SUMMIT, 3.7 *m.* (11,245 alt.), and SUMMIT CABIN. Until recently, adequate shelter from storms and protection for over-night campers has been afforded by the cabin, built by Lije Coalman for the Forest Service in 1915 as a summer fire lookout station. Buffeted by many storms, this small frame structure is today none too secure and threatens collapse. A registration book provided by the Mazamas is signed by all who make the crest. A few experts have made the climb in four hours.

ROUTE 2

Cloud Cap Inn or Tilly Jane Forest Camp—Ghost Ridge—Eliot Glacier—Cooper Spur—"The Chimney"—Summit; 3.8 m., Cooper Spur Climb.

Most popular north side route; comparatively safe; time, 7 hours.

One of the shortest of the charted ascents, this route is frequently chosen for such mass climbs as that of the Hood River Post of the American Legion. The climb begins either at the CLOUD CAP INN or the TILLY JANE FOREST CAMP, 0 *m.*, which is also the Legion base camp. At a point just below timberline complete camp and kitchen facilities are maintained for the large crowds that visit this section each July, either to participate in the annual Legion event of peak scaling or to join in the festivities of that occasion.

The trail ascends GHOST RIDGE, 1.2 *m.* (7,000 alt.), so-called for the ghostly trees left standing by an early forest fire, and proceeds along the easterly margin of ELIOT GLACIER, Mount Hood's largest and most characteristic ice mass. This crevasse-furrowed ice sheet was named for Dr. Thomas Lamb Eliot, an early north side mountaineer and one of Portland's well-known clergymen.

From this point, by a series of traverses, the way mounts the rocky ice-hung pitch of COOPER SPUR, 3 *m.* on the northeast shoulder of the mountain. In 1886 Mr. and Mrs. David Cooper operated a summer camp for vacationists on the wooded slopes just below this prominent feature.

Atop Cooper Spur (8,500 alt.) the route curves to the right, past TIE-IN ROCK, 3.2 *m.*, and climbs rapidly over a 45° snow slope to the "CHIMNEY," 3.3 *m.*, where a thousand feet of five-eighths inch rope or "lifeline" extends almost to the summit. (*Rope strung by the Hood River Crag Rats each May and removed after Labor Day. When not in use, rope coil is stored in Summit Cabin.*)

The SUMMIT, 3.8 *m.*, is the high north rim of the crater.

ROUTE 3

Tilly Jane Forest Camp—Eliot Glacier—Jefferson Rocks—
Cathedral Spire—Summit; 5 m., Sunshine Trail or North Face
Climb.

Rather steep but frequently favored for large parties; time, 9 hours.

This is the third most used route to the summit and was
developed in 1925 by Mark Weygandt. It is considered longer
and steeper than most of the peak climbs, but is generally a
safe route for large parties, and is so named because climbers
are in the direct light of the sun nearly all the way. Annually,
parties of Mazamas climb by this way because Eliot Glacier
is one of the most scenic and accessible glaciers in the world.
The Legion climbers have also followed this course.

The route originates at TILLY JANE FOREST CAMP, 0 *m.*,
just below Cooper Spur, and follows the Cooper Spur Trail
to ELIOT GLACIER, 3 *m.*, which it crosses. LANGILLE CRAGS,
a pinnacle wedge of rocks named for the peak-climbing Langilles, extends along the west side of the glacier. The way
angles up to JEFFERSON ROCKS, named for President Jefferson,
and HORSESHOE ROCK, 3.5 *m.* (8,700 alt.).

From this point the trail climbs at a 45° slant to the snow
and ice ridges north of the summit, where it rounds to
CATHEDRAL CRAGS, 4.5 *m.* (9,224 alt.), at the head of CATHEDRAL
RIDGE just above COE GLACIER. This ice field was named for
Captain Henry Coe, a pioneer resident of the Hood River
Valley. In the late eighties and nineties he operated a stage
line to the Cloud Cap district. From this ridge the climber
looks down (R) on Ladd, Sandy, and Reid Glaciers, and Eden
Park and the Wy'east Basin. Every type of glacial formation
is visible from this part of the trail.

Climbing above the Crags, the route crosses through the
CRATER to the SUMMIT, 5 *m.*

ROUTE 4

Timberline Lodge—Palmer Glacier—White River Glacier—
Steel Cliff—Summit; 4.8 m., Wy'east Trail Climb or Steel Cliff
Route.

Somewhat difficult and not without hazards; the safest of the spectacular
sporting routes; time, 8 hours.

ASCENT OF THE PEAK

Blazed in 1932 by James Mount and Everett Darr, this climb has become the principal sporting route to the crest and is the most climbed new route. The mountaineer must beware of falling rock and ice fragments, which make the final ascent a hazardous but spectacular journey. It is believed that Dryer followed a variation of this route in his questionable ascent of 1854. Around 1890 it was used by the Langilles, who conducted parties around to it from the north side. The present route is a simplification of the early climbs.

Leaving TIMBERLINE LODGE, 0 *m.*, and proceeding over the conventional South Side Route to the head of PALMER GLACIER, 1.5 *m.*, the trail turns right, dropping down into and crossing the upper reaches of WHITE RIVER GLACIER. Ascending to the moraine just east of this ice mass and below the rock rampart of STEEL CLIFF, 3 *m.*, it mounts a sheer snowfield to the lower cliff ridge, 3.4 *m.* Climbing this, the traveler looks directly down into the low southern portion of the CRATER and across to Crater Rock. Vertical pinnacles rise and drop on all sides and give a graphic picture of the formation of the peak.

From the WEST RIM OF THE CLIFF WALL, 3.6 *m.*, the route leads north up some tricky ledges of rotten rock. (*Climb at your own risk.*)

The climb finishes in a very steep 50° snow-filled "CHIMNEY," 4.3 *m.*, leading to the SUMMIT, 4.8 *m.*

ROUTE 5

Junction with Timberline Trail—Newton Clark Glacier—East Rim of Crater—Summit; 4.5 m., Newton Clark Glacier—East Face Climb.

Sheer and difficult; requires thorough knowledge of climbing hazards; time, 9 hours.

From a junction with the TIMBERLINE TRAIL, 0 *m.*, on the east side of the peak, this difficult route leads directly to the foot of NEWTON CLARK GLACIER. Newton Clark came to the Hood River Valley in 1877. A teacher, surveyor, and nature lover, he was the first to climb to the summit over this ice field, since named for him. As early as 1889 climbing parties were being conducted from the Cloud Cap area across Newton Clark Glacier to the spur below Steel Cliff, which they ascended.

Traversing this expansive white slope, the route reaches the sheer rock wall at the glacier's head, 3.8 *m.* Up this the way mounts. The extremely sharp faces and rotten rock formations of this upreared wall make a thorough knowledge of mountain hazards an essential. (*Climb at your own risk.*)

Only a few have made this ascent, which continues from the crest or EAST RIM OF THE CRATER, 4.2 *m.* to the SUMMIT, 4.5 *m.*

ROUTE 6

Upper Sandy River Canyon—Yocum Ridge—Sandy Glacier—Reid Glacier—Illumination Rock—Summit; 4.8 m., West Face Climb or "Avalanche Route."

A route of some danger due to frequent slides; time, 9 hours.

This route, constantly endangered by snow and rock slides, mounts the pumice slopes of the SANDY RIVER CANYON. From a junction with the TIMBERLINE TRAIL, 0 *m.*, it follows along the north face of YOCUM RIDGE, 2 *m.*, named for Oliver C. Yocum, who came to Oregon as a boy in the emigration of 1847. Prior to 1900 he led more climbers to the top of Mount Hood than any other guide. SANDY GLACIER lies white and glaring to the climber's left as he ascends.

At the head of the Ridge the route crosses REID GLACIER, 3 *m.* (8,136 alt.), at its extreme tip. Following the visit in 1901 of Professor Henry Fielding Reid, an authority on glaciers of Johns Hopkins University, this lesser ice mass was named for him. ILLUMINATION ROCK (9,580 alt.) stands to the right. On this prominent eminence was staged the first artificial illumination of Mount Hood.

From this point the route climbs eastward almost directly up the steep rugged slope to the crest of the summit ridge. (*Climb at your own risk.*)

The route is completed at the SUMMIT, 4.8 *m.*

ASCENT OF THE PEAK

ROUTE 7

Eden Park—Junction with Timberline Trail—Ladd Glacier
—Cathedral Ridge—Summit; 6 m., Cathedral Ridge Climb.

Arduous and extremely dangerous; avalanche conditions prevail; time,
11 hours.

First explored by Newton Clark in 1887, this route leaves
the TIMBERLINE TRAIL, 0 *m.*, in the EDEN PARK area.
Climbing over small EDEN PARK GLACIER it proceeds (R)
across the snowfield of LADD GLACIER, so named for William
Mead Ladd of Portland, who at an early date did much to
make the north side section a recreational center.

The way mounts to the rocky buttress of CATHEDRAL RIDGE,
3 *m.* (9,500 alt.), climbing that long almost perpendicular face
to its CREST, 5 *m.* En route the climber stares down (L) at the
tip end of PULPIT ROCK, a sharp and solitary pinnacle at the
head of Ladd and Coe Glaciers. (*Climb at your own risk.*)

From this dividing ridge, free of snow only in mid-summer,
the route—which at this point offers several variations—
ranges southeast, mounting by the Sunshine Route over the
steep final grade to the snow crags of the SUMMIT, 6 *m.*

ROUTE 8

Wy'east Basin—Ladd Glacier—Barrett Spur—Coe Rock—
Cathedral Ridge—Summit; 5.5 m., Pulpit Rock Climb.

Extremely difficult, with many hazards; alternates from rock to ice; time,
9 hours.

Diverging from the TIMBERLINE TRAIL, 0 *m.*, in the
WY'EAST BASIN just below LADD GLACIER, this hazardous route
climbs over the northern ice fields and along the slopes of
BARRETT SPUR, 1.7 *m.* (7,846 alt.). This ridge dividing Coe from
Ladd Glaciers was named for Doctor P. G. Barrett, who settled in Hood River Valley in 1871. For many years he was the
only physician in a wide region of ranches and wilderness.

At 3.2 *m.* the route mounts to a junction with LADD GLACIER
and COE ROCK (8,705 alt). Here the route continues up the
rock cleaver between LADD and COE GLACIERS, sometimes forc-
ing the mountaineer to the steep ice of Coe, because of im-

103

passible rock. The great lava nose of PULPIT ROCK, 4.2 *m.*, rears between Ladd and Coe Glaciers just below the merger point of these two upslanted ice sheets. In 1887 a party headed by Newton Clark climbed along the west side of this rock, but the sheer east face was not conquered until 1936, by Irving B. Lincoln. (*Climb at your own risk.*)

From a junction with the CREST OF CATHEDRAL RIDGE, 5 *m.*, the trail follows the conventional Sunshine Route to the SUMMIT, 5.5 *m.*

ROUTE 9

Timberline Lodge—Lone Fir Lookout—Palmer Glacier— Crater Rock—East Crater Wall—Steel Cliff—Summit; 4.6 m., Inner Steel Cliff or East Face of Crater Wall Climb.

Rocky and insecure; requires delicate hand and footholds; time, 10 hours.

Leaving TIMBERLINE LODGE and the Timberline Trail, 0 *m.*, this hazardous climb, made first by Gary Leach in 1937, follows the conventional South Side Route to the foot of STEEL CLIFF, 3.2 *m.*, near the HOT ROCKS.

The route up the face of Steel Cliff, inside the cup of the crater, traverses an area of scattered and loose lava rock, that readily assumes an avalanche nature. The most secure foot and handholds are imperative. (*Climb at your own risk.*)

Topping Steel Cliff, 4.2 *m.* (11,000 alt.), the white crown of the SUMMIT, 4.6 *m.* stands a short distance to the north.

ROUTE 10

Paradise Park—Illumination Rock—Reid Glacier—Yocum Ridge—The Crest—Summit; 7 m., Sandy Glacier Cirque or Headwall Climb.

The mountain's second most difficult climb; for experts only; time, 10 hours.

This extremely difficult climb, first made in 1937 by Joe Leuthold and Russell McJury, is up the mountain's west face, leaving the Timberline Trail at PARADISE PARK, 0 *m.*, on the southwest side.

Emerging from the highest-reaching trees, the way crosses ZIGZAG GLACIER, 1.5 *m.*, and climbs up to the saddle above ILLUMINATION ROCK, 3.2 *m.* This isolated mass of abrupt proportions and difficult ascent, was first conquered by T. Raymond Conway in the early twenties. From this point the way crosses the upper ice of REID GLACIER, 4.1 *m.*, to the head of YOCUM RIDGE, 4.8 *m.*

From this ridge the route works up the precipitous rock wall that stands at the head of SANDY GLACIER, 5.5 *m.* The climb becomes extremely difficult owing to the disintegrating nature of the cliff up which it mounts. Constant peril is occasioned because of the active rock slides. (*Climb at your own risk.*)

At the CREST, 6.5 *m.*, the climber literally straddles the narrow ridge. The way continues to the SUMMIT, 7 *m.*

ROUTE 11

Tilly Jane Forest Camp—Cooper Spur—Eliot Glacier Headwall—Summit; 3.5 m., Eliot Glacier or Headwall Climb.

Extremely hazardous; for experts willing to take a chance; time, 10 hours.

Rated as the most difficult of the climbs to the summit is this route up the northeast shoulder of the mountain. Only three parties have been able to make this ascent, first climbed by Mark Weygandt and Arthur Emmons in the early twenties.

Leaving Timberline Trail and TILLY JANE FOREST CAMP, 0 *m.*, the way lies exactly between the Cooper Spur Route (L) and the Sunshine Route (R). Proceeding over ELIOT GLACIER, 1.5 *m.* to the HEADWALL, 2.6 *m.*, the mountaineer must mount this nearly perpendicular, craggy surface, which lifts almost 3,000 feet overhead.

The climb up this sheer wall can only be made when there is sufficient snow and ice to hold the rotten lava rock in place. Expert axe work and rare judgment are required, particularly at places where the overhanging ledge subjects the climber to extreme hazard. (*Climb at your own risk.*)

Once on the CREST OF THE HEADWALL, 3.2 *m.*, the way is up the short remaining but steep slope to the SUMMIT, 3.5 *m.*

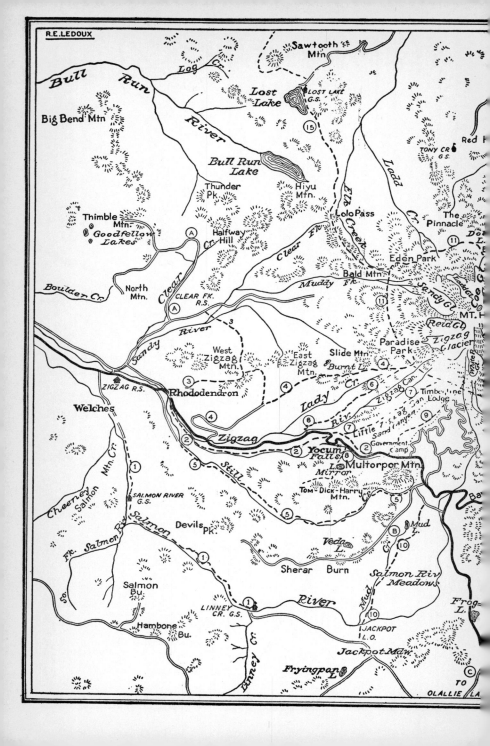

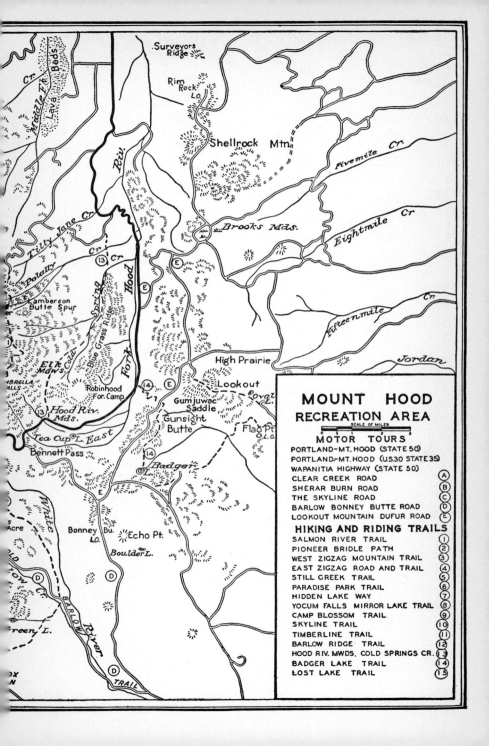

MOUNT HOOD
RECREATION AREA

SCALE OF MILES

MOTOR TOURS
PORTLAND-MT. HOOD (STATE 50)
PORTLAND-MT. HOOD (U.S. 30 STATE 35)
WAPANITIA HIGHWAY (STATE 50)
CLEAR CREEK ROAD — Ⓐ
SHERAR BURN ROAD — Ⓑ
THE SKYLINE ROAD — Ⓒ
BARLOW BONNEY BUTTE ROAD — Ⓓ
LOOKOUT MOUNTAIN DUFUR ROAD — Ⓔ

HIKING AND RIDING TRAILS
SALMON RIVER TRAIL — ①
PIONEER BRIDLE PATH — ②
WEST ZIGZAG MOUNTAIN TRAIL — ③
EAST ZIGZAG ROAD AND TRAIL — ④
STILL CREEK TRAIL — ⑤
PARADISE PARK TRAIL — ⑥
HIDDEN LAKE WAY — ⑦
YOCUM FALLS MIRROR LAKE TRAIL — ⑧
CAMP BLOSSOM TRAIL — ⑨
SKYLINE TRAIL — ⑩
TIMBERLINE TRAIL — ⑪
BARLOW RIDGE TRAIL — ⑫
HOOD RIV. MWDS. COLD SPRINGS CR. — ⑬
BADGER LAKE TRAIL — ⑭
LOST LAKE TRAIL — ⑮

Winter Sports and Ski Trails

IN the years just prior to Oregon settlement, trappers lived in winter-bound cabins in the remote Cascades, a few as high as timberline on the taller peaks. At a later period, settlers came to the meadows, where the snows of winter nearly or completely covered their rude log homes and rough board structures. In those early days, and until quite recent years, the winter trip to Mount Hood from Portland was an extremely difficult one, and infrequently taken. Either of two courses was followed, and both were time-consuming journeys. One was by team and wagon up the Barlow Road, as far as the deepening snows permitted, with the remainder of the way to Government Camp made on snowshoes. The other route was by train to Hood River, thence by stage up the valley as far as the straining horses could plow through the huge drifts of the higher slopes and canyons. Here likewise snowshoes and physical stamina were needed for completing the journey to such north side shelters as Cloud Cap Inn and the few settlers' lodges. On such occasions travelers went warmly wrapped in furs, and copious publicity preceded and followed each outing.

It is believed that Dick Maupin, active as a forest ranger about 1900, was the first to use skis as a means of winter travel on Mount Hood. This was in the Summit Prairie region. Shortly afterward, in 1903, the Mazamas held their pioneer winter outing. Setting forth on what was then called "a perilous trip," this party of three—Colonel Hawkins, T. Brook White, and Martin W. Gorman, the botanist, on "Norwegian skis" and using "balancing poles," climbed high up the white peak. On this outing Mr. White prophesied that the time would come when more people would come to Mount Hood in winter for the sports than ever came in summer. "The aspect of the mountain is infinitely finer than in summer," he declared.

The Oregonian

SKIERS

The Oregonian

SKIERS

THE SKI JUMPER LEAVING THE TAKE-OFF

CLIMBING MT. HOOD BY WAY OF STEEL CLIFF

APPLYING GREASE PAINT TO PREVENT SUNBURNING   *U. S. Forest Service*

McIntosh   LOOKOUT CABIN ON SUMMIT OF MT. HOOD

TERMINUS OF NEWTON
CLARK GLACIER

Onthank

CLIMBING THE ICE FALLS,
ELIOT GLACIER

Ijames

RIDING PARTY

Timberline Lodge Ass'n.

U. S. Forest Service

CAMPING

PUNCH BOWL FALLS, EAGLE CREEK TRAIL

ALONG THE OLD STAGE ROAD, NEAR MT. HOOD

MT. HOOD, VIEWED FROM CLOUD CAP INN
(6000 *Feet Elevation*)

Altorf

SOUTH SLOPE OF MT. HOOD IN SUMMER

Among the winter recreationists visiting the north side annually from 1901 to 1909 was a group that organized the Portland Snowshoe Club. These clubmen used Norwegian-made skis. In 1910 they built a mountain cabin on Ghost Ridge near timberline, a comfortable structure still in use as a clubhouse. The Portland Ski Club was formed in 1907, and annual February trips to Government Camp were begun. Their entire purpose was skiing. Of the Mazamas that came each year in adventurous numbers, only the hardier members climbed beyond the end of the road at Rhododendron. As a means of winter security the Mazama Club built a lodge at the foot of Laurel Hill, near what is now Twin Bridges. From this point club members climbed on skis to Paradise Park, and the west and south slopes of the higher altitudes. This was in 1920. About this time the Mount Hood Loop Highway went through to Government Camp and, when in 1926 the Highway Department began plowing out the snow-choked thoroughfare, the multitude of winter sports enthusiasts followed. With winter road clearance assured, the center of skiing moved to the Government Camp area. And the Mazama Lodge moved with it, up the mountain.

Only within the past ten years have winter sports on Mount Hood become the popular diversion of the many. Not until after the winter of 1926-27, in which Calvin White, a sixteen-year-old skier disappeared in a storm and nearly lost his life were efforts made to make winter recreation a safe sport. In 1927 the Advertising Club of Portland sponsored the development of a national sports playground in the area east and south of Government Camp, where a ski-jumping hill was prepared, a toboggan slide graded, and a small running area cleared. This centering of winter activities was done with the intention of keeping the sports of the snow season within a comparatively small and safe sector. Despite this, the more ardent skiers were soon climbing to timberline and far above. A few ascended on skis to the very summit, from which they made a precipitate return. By 1930 the sport enthusiasts had taken the white mountain.

The first ski hill was down the east slope of Multorpor Mountain just west of Swim. Here the first jumping tournament was held. Soon a "master" hill was graded on Multorpor's north slope, and the Mount Hood Ski Club was formed.

This soon became the Cascade Ski Club, and a club house was built. When later a northwest unit of the National Ski Association was formed, this club and other local groups became participators in ski events of local, regional, and national scope. Likewise, the Portland Winter Sports Association was organized to popularize winter sports on Hood, and an annual carnival program became an event appealing to thousands. Only within the last few years has the program expanded to include the popular downhill and slalom racing.

Meanwhile, the Ski Bowl on the north slopes of Tom-Dick-Harry Mountain was cleared for the sport of the waxed runners. An enlarged area of more than 160 acres, offering all degrees of slope and all types of skiing conditions, was also put into use in the space lying between the Ski Bowl and the Ski Jump. At once this became—and still is—the ideal training field for amateurs.

Only in comparatively recent years has the upper ski area come into general usage. The Alpine and Blossom Ski Trails were traced adventurously down the mountainside. The Nanitch Ski Hill, a well-cleared portion having a variety of general and "stunt" features, came into popularity. Free of snags, with a varying terrain, it proved suitable for all degrees of ability. With the construction of the two Timberline Roads, this upper skiing area greatly increased in appeal. In 1937 the construction and opening of Timberline Lodge, at the head of this vast sport's field, brought an added multitude of recreationists. To accommodate these, coming in greatest numbers on weekends and holidays, extensive parking sectors were allotted to cars, at Timberline Lodge, Phlox Point, Summit Ranger Station and Government Camp.

The open and wooded slopes below Cooper Spur, on the north shoulder of Mount Hood, were in 1938 prepared as a ski area. Winter sports seekers from the north enter this district by way of the Mount Hood Loop Highway and the Cooper Spur Road. While the upper slopes as far up the mountain as the Tilly Jane Forest Camp are used by the more hardy and daring skiers, the central ski area, with full advantages for both the expert and the novice, lies to the right of the ascending Cooper Spur Road just above its junction with the Loop Highway.

With the growing popularity of skiing, interest in winter

110

hiking on snowshoes has also increased. At least a few sports lovers tramp long distances on this webbed and durable footwear, especially serviceable in snow too soft to properly support the more customary skis. Long-experienced skiers occasionally climb within a thousand feet of the very summit of winter-wrapped Mount Hood, from which they "schuss" rapidly back to more friendly levels. These and many others also find Paradise Park, with its open east and west slopes, a "natural" skiing range.

Latest in the sport's development on the mountain is the construction by the Forest Service of an upper ski tow, or lift, so built as to be out of view from Timberline Lodge.

Today the skiing fields of Mount Hood are the most heavily used in America, with more than 75,000 sports seekers in the snow season of 1938-39. Each year such tournaments as the National Downhill Championship Meet, the Northwest Jumping Meet, and the Grand Slalom Races are held with many thrills and spills. These events occur in the mountain's upper and lower sectors, on the south side.

On these upper slopes, a ski patrol, begun in the winter of 1937 and conducted as an altruistic first aid enterprise, covers the regular courses at intervals. Down each trail at darkfall, two-man units descend to the highway, assisting any who may have met with accident, thus avoiding any possibility of tragedy.

SKIING AREAS AND TRAILS

Special Information for Skiers: Skiers should be warmly but not too heavily clad in garments that permit free bodily movement. Skis should be of manageable length and weight and secured to shoes of stout leather. Skiers should carry ski poles or alpenstocks, should wear smoked glasses to protect the eyes from the blinding effect of sun on snow, and should protect the skin from wind and sunburn.

While the skiing areas of Mount Hood afford a variety of practice slopes, all the regular trails are fast. To use these safely a knowledge of skiing is necessary and the timely use of such maneuvers as stemming and stem turning to slow the descent over rough and dangerous terrain. Sane skiing calls for the selection of trails suitable to ability. Once control is lost the skier should not hesitate to fall immediately; further momentum only adds to the danger of a severe fall or accident.

Show due regard to trail conditions. Do not attempt to ski when the snow is shallow or icy. However "powder snow," although it makes travel slow and difficult, is safe. Ideal skiing is over well-firmed snow without crust.

Heed the advice of officials and patrolmen (*recognized by Forest Service badge*) as to proper trails. When descending a trail the skier should call "track!" This gives him the right of way and cautions others to give clearance. The skier should not stand idly or walk on the ski trails.

When tired stop skiing immediately; do not be too proud to walk. Should a skier become completely exhausted he should be kept warm as possible and a ski patrol toboggan sent for. If a skier is injured summon the ski patrol.

Do not run trails after sundown, when they usually become icy and consequently very "fast," materially increasing the danger of accidents. An injured skier, if on a late run, may not be found by the ski patrol.

Skiers should stay on the trails and within the prescribed skiing areas. He should never go alone into unfrequented country. Do not attempt the hazardous.

Watch the weather. Mount Hood winter climate is variable and storms often arise suddenly which necessitates a constant vigil. If storms threaten the skier should remain within easy reach of a shelter.

SKI BOWL—SKI RACING TRAIL—SLALOM COURSE.

Junction with State 50—Tom-Dick-Harry Mountain Trail; 0.5 m. Class AA and A Area; 230 acres.

The SKI BOWL, a natural three-sided area with slopes ranging from 30 to 50 degrees, is on the north flank of Tom-Dick-Harry Mountain. Its open slopes provide ideal conditions for slalom racing and its level floor, one-fourth mile square, is a junction point for several trails from the crests above and from the Central Skiing Area (*see below*) to the east. A continuous rope Ski Tow lifts passengers for 400 feet up the 900 foot rise of the abrupt south wall of the bowl. Ski instruction available during weekends. There is a ski hut for rewaxing and rest, and a first aid station.

A curving, fast SKI RACING TRAIL, two miles long, starts from the Tom-Dick-Harry Lookout Station on the ridge above, and sloping east and north skirts the west edge of the bowl. Rating, expert.

NATIONAL SLALOM CHAMPIONSHIP COURSE descends Tom-Dick-Harry Mountain in a corkscrew fashion and terminates in the Ski Bowl. This trail is one-half mile long and has a drop of 800 feet. Rating, expert.

CASCADE SKI JUMP—CENTRAL SKIING AREA.

Junction with State 50 at Government Camp (R) on Multorpor Mountain Trail, 0.4 m.

Class AA and A area; 800 acres.

The CASCADE SKI JUMP, built in 1928 by the Cascade Ski Club and improved in 1931, descends the long and spectacular north slope of Multorpor Mountain (4,857 alt.). Three jumps are provided: distances of 200 to 300 feet are possible from the Class A jump; 150 feet from the Class B jump; and up to 100 feet from the Class C jump. It is open only to qualified jumpers and is the scene of many annual ski-jumping events of national importance. A small fee is charged spectators on tournament days. Two ski tows of the rope type convey skiers 700 feet up the jumping slope. A shelter cabin stands at the crest of the hill.

The CENTRAL SKIING AREA, a 300-acre snowfield of moderate practice grades, lies along the north slopes of the ridgeway between Multorpor Mountain and Tom-Dick-Harry Mountain. There is a connecting trail with the Ski Bowl, on the west.

There is a diverging trail, three-fourths mile long, from Multorpor Mountain to Summit Guard Station.

Originating at various points, a variety of trails and runs diverge throughout the area.

SUMMIT MEADOWS SKI TRAIL.

State 50 to Summit Guard Station, 0.2 m.

Class B area; 10 acres.

SUMMIT MEADOWS SKI TRAIL follows the varying levels of the old Barlow Road, curving southeast. It is three-fourths of a mile long and is rated an easy course for beginners. Training in ski technic can be acquired on this trail before the more difficult runs are attempted. First aid equipment at the Summit Guard Station.

GLADE SKI TRAIL—BLOSSOM SKI TRAIL—ALPINE SKI TRAIL—NANITCH SKI AREA—CASCADE SKI TRAIL—MAZAMA HILL AND SKI TRAIL—WEST LEG SKI TRAIL.

Timberline Lodge—Timberline Cabin—Phlox Point—Nanitch Hill—Mazama Hill—Government Camp—Summit Guard Station.
Class AA and A area; 700 acres.

GLADE SKI TRAIL starts from the open glades lying between Timberline Lodge (*first aid station*) and Timberline Cabin and strikes down the mountain through a wide burned-off area, following the eastern margin of Sand Canyon. At about the 4,400 level it curves to the right, connecting with the Blossom Ski Trail (*see below*) and the Cascade Ski Trail (*see below*), terminating at Government Camp (*first aid station*). From an altitude of 6,000 feet this route drops by moderate grades to the 3,875 foot level, a distance of four miles. Rating, intermediate.

BLOSSOM SKI TRAIL, starting at Timberline Lodge, drops through scattered trees and in a run of three miles descends 2,200 feet. Combines with Glade Trail one mile from terminus.

Thrills such as those found on famous courses in the Alps are common on this course; to negotiate the route successfully requires the skill and nerve of an expert.

ALPINE SKI TRAIL takes off from a point just west of Timberline Lodge and drops 2,000 feet in a little less than four miles; a fast 15-minute run. It ends just west of the Summit Guard Station on the Loop Highway. Features of this course are the "Corkscrew Canyon" and the "Washboard." Rating, intermediate.

Midway on the Alpine Ski Trail is the NANITCH SKI AREA and just below it is Mazama Hill, each offering a variety of practice slopes. About 40 acres are cleared of all snags and irregularities, affording facilities for slalom and downhill training. These areas may also be entered from the West Leg Timberline Road at a point one and one-half miles above the Loop Highway.

CASCADE SKI TRAIL separates from the Alpine Ski Trail in the Nanitch Ski Area, and continues south and west down Mazama Hill. It connects with the Blossom Trail at a point just above its terminus with the Loop Highway. This course, one and one-half miles long, is 60 feet wide and has a maximum grade of 25 per cent. Rating, intermediate.

MAZAMA SKI TRAIL diverges from the Alpine Trail on Mazama Hill, and courses southeast, downhill to the Mazama Lodge, a distance of one mile. Rating, intermediate.

WEST LEG SKI TRAIL starts from South or Poochie Glade below Timberline Lodge, and ends at the Loop Highway near the Summit Guard Station. It is a run of about six miles, with many easy curves; the last half of it is over the Old Timberline Road. This route 50 feet wide, has a drop of 2,300 feet over an 8 per cent grade. Rating, novice. This trail is also used for snowshoeing.

LONE FIR SKI TRAIL — NATIONAL DOWNHILL CHAMPIONSHIP TRAIL—TOBOGGAN COURSE.

Timberline Lodge to Lone Fir Lookout Station, 1 m.
Class AA area 300 feet.

LONE FIR SKI TRAIL, a fast slalom course, starts from Lone Fir Lookout (*shelter, first aid station*), at an altitude of 6,700 feet, and terminates one mile below in the glades immediately west of Timberline Lodge. Some daring experts extend this run by climbing to Crater Rock and from an elevation of 9,500 feet descend through the glades to the Loop Highway, using either the Blossom Trail or the Alpine Trail. Covering this combined route, a drop of 5,600 feet in six and one half miles is experienced.

NATIONAL DOWNHILL CHAMPIONSHIP TRAIL or "Turtleneck" is for experts of exceptional ability only, and is extremely hazardous and fast. Starting at Crater Rock, this course sweeps down the upper ridgeway between Salmon and White Rivers, descending over a concluding 50 per cent grade into the Salmon River canyon just east of Timberline Lodge.

This is an altitude drop of nearly 4,500 feet in a distance of two and three-fourths miles.

A Ski Lift extends from a point 200 yards east of Timberline Lodge to a terminus well above Lone Fir Lookout, a distance of one and one-tenth miles. Its capacity is 300 skiers per hour with a chair every 12 seconds.

A TOBOGGAN COURSE at the rear of Timberline Lodge is operated by the Wy'east Climbers and is open to the public so long as certain rules are obeyed.

COOPER SPUR SKI TRAILS—SKI BOWL—SKI JUMPING HILL—SAND CANYON RIDGE—BEAR MOUNTAIN—PRACTICE SLOPE.

Junction with State 35 at Cooper Spur Road, 0.3 m.
Class A and B area; 250 acres.

COOPER SPUR SKI JUMPING HILL, centered in this area, affords two leaps: Class A jump, a leap of 250 feet; Class B jump, a leap of 75 feet. Both jumps descend into the Ski Bowl, a 40-acre area cleared of all trees and obstacles. Rating, qualified experts.

Class A Slalom Course descends from the Ski Jumping Hill, two miles, to Sand Canyon. Rating, expert.

Class B Downhill Run starts from the Ski Jumping Hill and terminates at the Homestead Inn and the Cooper Spur Road, distance one mile. Rating, intermediate.

A rope tow owned and operated by the Mount Hood Ski Club, conveys skiers from the Ski Bowl to the crest of the Ski Jumping Hill. Centrally located in the Bowl is a shelter cabin with a large stone fireplace.

Class A Downhill Run, two miles long, descends from the Sand Canyon Ridge and terminates at the Homestead Inn. Rating, expert.

Class B Slalom Course, one mile long, sweeps over the upper grades of the area and comes to an end one-fourth mile west of Cooper Spur Inn and the Spur Road. Rating, intermediate.

The PRACTICE AREA, affording a variety of grades for the novice, lies on the slopes of nearby Bear Mountain.

Adventurous experts climb the mountain slopes to the Tilly Jane Forest Camp area and ski back through the trees, a distance of four miles to the Ski Bowl.

Long-distance skiing is provided over the Cross-Country Ski Trail, which runs from the Ski Bowl to Parkdale, 10 miles north.

Running from the Ski Jumping Hill to Sand Canyon, a Toboggan Course is for the use of all who furnish their own coasting equipment.

PART III

Appendices

Chronology

1792   Oct. 30—Mount Hood first sighted by white men. Members of the crew of H.M.S. *Chatham* under command of Lieutenant William R. Broughton while exploring the Columbia River saw a "very remarkable high mountain" which Lieutenant Broughton named after his patron, Rear Admiral Samuel Hood of the Royal British Navy.

1805   Oct. 21—Mount Hood sighted by Lewis and Clark who called it "the Timm or Falls mountain," because of its proximity to the great falls of the Columbia.

1825   David Douglas, Scotch botanist of the Royal British Horticultural Society, visited the Columbia River valley. At that time he expressed the opinion that Mount Hood could not be scaled.

1843   Oct. 23—Captain John C. Fremont, on an exploring expedition into the Oregon Country sighted Mount Hood from a spur of the Blue Mountains 180 miles away.

1845   Oct.-Dec.—The Samuel Barlow and Joel Palmer wagon trains blazed first road over the Cascade Range just south of Mount Hood.

1845   Oct. 12—Joel Palmer climbed far up the south slope of Mount Hood, the first man to climb any distance up the white peak.

1846   Barlow received a franchise from the Provisional Government of Oregon and began construction of a toll road over the route his train had followed the previous year. By August the road was sufficiently completed to handle the immigrant travel of that year.

1849   "The government camp in the mountains" was established by Lieutenant William Frost when forced to abandon his wagons here while on a military expedition.

1854   Thomas J. Dryer, editor of the *Oregonian*, claimed to have reached the summit of Mount Hood, but his claim was discredited by later investigators.

1857   July 11—A party consisting of Henry L. Pittock, Rev. T. A. Woods, Lyman Chittenden, and Wilbur Cornell, made the first authenticated climb to the summit of Mount Hood.

1859   Aug. 20—The Portland *Weekly Oregonian* reported spectacular volcanic activity and "intermittent columns of fire" emanating from the crater on Mount Hood for two hours.

1867   Miss Mary Robinson and Miss Fanny Case were the first women to reach the summit of Mount Hood.

1868   Perry Vickers built Summit House at Summit Meadows on the old Barlow Road.

1870   July 4—The first attempted illumination of the mountain by Perry Vickers who built a large bonfire there. It could not be seen from Portland (*see July 4, 1887*).

APPENDICES

1873 July 4—Perry Vickers was first man to spend the night on the summit of Mount Hood. He set off fireworks for the benefit of "a committee of 25 persons of unimpeachable veracity."

1877 July 4—A party of men from The Dalles made an unsuccessful attempt to illuminate the mountain.

1883-84 The first road from Hood River to the north timberline of Mount Hood was constructed.

1884 First camping resort was established on Tilly Jane creek by Mrs. Dave Cooper. The site was on Cooper Spur, just below the present Cloud Cap Inn.

1885 July 4—A fourth unsuccessful try at illuminating Mount Hood was attempted by a group of Portland men armed with a large supply of red fire and a device to set it off. The "infernal machine" operated prematurely igniting the fire in midafternoon.

1887 July 4—Mount Hood finally illuminated successfully by a party of seven men led by Will Steel. One hundred pounds of red fire were used and the result was seen from many far distant towns and villages.

1887 Sept. 14—The first mountaineering group in Oregon, the Oregon Alpine Club, was organized. It suspended activities upon the organization of the Mazamas in 1894 (see below).

1889 Cloud Cap Inn was erected of Amabilis fir logs at timberline on the northeast shoulder of Mount Hood.

1892 June 17—President Harrison, by proclamation, created the Bull Run Timberland Reserve.

1892 Sept.—G. W. Graham and W. A. Langille made the first trip afoot around the mountain, starting their hike from the north side.

1893 Sept. 28—The Cascade Forest Reserve was created by the Federal Government.

1894 July 19—The Mazamas, famous Oregon mountain club was organized on the summit of Mount Hood, by 200 men and women who became charter members of the club. Membership is confined to those who have climbed to the summit of a snow peak on which there is a living glacier, and which cannot be reached except on foot.

1897 July 11—The first death on Mount Hood was that of Frederic Kern, a 60-year-old Swiss grocer of Portland, who attempted to climb the peak alone and was swept over a cliff by an avalanche.

1897 Elijah Coalman, at the age of 15, began a long career as Mount Hood's best-known and best-loved summit guide.

1900 First resort hotel on the mountain built at Government Camp by O. C. Yocum.

1907 A. H. Sylvester, in charge of a mapping party of the U. S. Geological Survey, made the first survey of the Mount Hood quadrangle.

1907 The Portland Ski Club was organized. Their sole object was skiing and annual trips were made to Government Camp in February for that purpose.

1908 July 1—The Oregon National Forest was carved from the Cascade National Forest.

1911-12 First "Government Camp Hotel" was erected by Elijah Coalman.

1915 Elijah Coalman built a cabin for the Forest Service on the summit of Mount Hood. For a number of years it served as a fire lookout station and shelter house for climbers who reached the top of the mountain.

1919   Barlow Toll Road was deeded by Henry Wemme through his attorney, George W. Joseph, to the State of Oregon.

1919   First work was begun on the modern Mount Hood Loop Highway, two miles west of Government Camp.

1924   Jan. 21—Mount Hood National Forest was created out of the Oregon National Forest.

1926   April 28—Mount Hood Recreation Area was created and defined. There were 83,731 acres set aside for this purpose.

1926   The Hood River Crag Rats, a mountaineering club of Hood River, was organized. Members must be experienced climbers and have expert first-aid knowledge.

1926   The Mount Hood Loop highway was completed and opened to the public.

1928   The Cascade Ski jump on Multorpor Hill was constructed. Three years later it was materially improved.

1929   The Federal government completed that part of the Wapinitia highway within the national forest at a cost of half a million dollars.

1930   Dec.—The Wy'east Climbers, a mountain climbing club was organized, with its membership limited to mountaineers of proved ability.

1931   Mount Hood Primitive area set aside by the U. S. Forest Service.

1936   June 14—Cornerstone laid for new Timberline Lodge.

1937   Sept. 28—Timberline Lodge, constructed by WPA, dedicated by President Franklin D. Roosevelt.

1938   Feb. 4—Timberline Lodge formally opened to the public.

Bibliography

Berreman, Joel V., *Tribal Distribution in Oregon*. No. 47, 1937. Supplement to *American Anthropologist*, Vol. 39, No. 3, Part 2.

Gabrielson, Ira N., *Western American Alpines*. The Macmillan Co., N. Y., 1932.

Haskins, Leslie R., *Wild Flowers of the Pacific Coast*. Metropolitan Press, Portland, 1934.

Judson, Katharine Berry, *Myths and Legends of the Pacific Northwest*. Chicago: A. C. McClurg & Co., 1910. Indian legends.

Lyman, William Denison, *The Columbia River*. New York: G. P. Putnam's Sons, 1918. A chapter on Mount Hood.

Mazama, The. Portland, Oregon: 1896-1940. Various authors. The annual, or last yearly number of this monthly, published by The Mazamas, a mountaineering club.

McNeil, Fred H., *Wy'east, 'The Mountain.'* Portland, Oregon: Metropolitan Press, 1937. A history of Mount Hood.

Oregon Out of Doors. Portland Oregon: The Mazamas, 1920. Various authors. A collection of articles, most of which treat of Mount Hood.

Rusk, C. E., *Tales of a Western Mountaineer*. Boston: Houghton, Mifflin Co. 1924. A chapter on "The Etherial Mountain."

Steel Points. Portland, Oregon: privately published, irregularly issued from 1906 to 1917. A variety of information on Mount Hood, gathered at first hand.

Steel, W. G., *The Mountains of Oregon*. David Steel, Pub., Portland, 1890.

Sudworth, George B., *Forest Trees of the Pacific Slope*. U. S. Forest Service, Washington, D. C.

Williams, John Harvey, *The Guardians of the Columbia*. Tacoma, Washington: privately published, 1912. A description of Mount Hood, with photographs.

Index

INDEX

INDEX

Gilman, Miss Esther, 93
Gladstone, 46
Gnarl Ridge, 82
Government Camp, 41, 53, 55, 56, 71, 76, 78, 108, 110
Graham, G. W., 42
Gray, Cornelius, 88
Gray, Robert, 36
Gresham, 46, 53
Gullickson, Glen, 93
Gumjuwac Saddle, 60, 69, 85

History, 23-44
Holman, George, 61
Homestead Inn, 59, 85
Hood, Rear-Admiral Samuel, 3, 37
Hood River American Legion Camp, 82
Hood River Crag Rats, 43
Hood River Meadows, 60, 83
Hood River Valley, 41, 58
Horseshoe Rock, 100
Horse Thief Meadows, 60
Hot Rocks, 98, 104
Hudson's Bay Company, 37

Illumination Point, 77
Illumination Rock, 87, 89, 102, 105
Indians: artifacts, 25-26; burial customs, 27-28; canoes, 25-26; clothing, 26; foods, 26-27; houses, 26; myths, 30-36; "pit" houses, 28-29; religious beliefs, 27-28
Indians: Warm Springs Reservation, 29, 62

Indian tribes, 23-36; Cayuse, 24; Celilos, 25; Chinooks, 25; Chinookan, 25; Clackamas, 25; Clowewalla, 25; Hood River, 24, 25, 27; Kushooks, 25; Molallas, 24, 28, 29; Piutes, 25, 29, 63; Sahaptin, 25; Salish, 25; Smackshops, 24, 25; Snakes, 25; Tenino, 24, 63; Tilkuni, 24; Tyghs, 24, 28, 29, 62; Warm Springs, 29, 59; Wasco, 12, 25, 29; Wishrams, 25
Inland Empire, 57

Jackpot Meadows, 79
Jefferson Rocks, 100
Joseph, George W., 41
Juniper Flat, 62

Kelly, Hall Jackson, 37
Kern, Frederic, 90
Killingsworth, Fay, 90
Killingsworth, William, 90

Ladd Glacier, 98, 103
Ladd, William S., 59, 103
Lakes: Badger, 5, 69, 85; Bull Run, 5, 41; Burnt, 76; Clackamas, 66; Dollar, 82; Frog, 5, 63; Hidden, 54, 77; Kinzel, 66; Lost Lake, 5, 30, 33, 41, 57, 76, 86; Mirror, 78; Mud, 79; Olallie, 20, 67; Trillium, 79; Veda, 66; Wahtum Lake, 86
Langille Crags, 100
Langille, Douglas, 90
Langille, James L., 59
Langille, W. A., 42

129

INDEX

INDEX

INDEX